Wings of the Dawn

Finding God Beyond Religion and Darwinism

And Making Sense of Bereavement

Peter McCormack

This book is dedicated to
Rachel,
who was and is and always will be,
one of the greatest loves of all of my lives, on earth, and forever.

"If I rise on the wings of the dawn,
if I settle on the far side of the sea,
even there your hand will guide me,
your right hand will hold me fast"
Psalm 139.

Special thanks to Wendy Zerbst of Queensland, Australia, healer and counsellor, who read my early manuscript, gave me invaluable advice, and gave me the confidence to go for publication.
Special thanks also to Lynda Sullivan, Belfast, who gave her time freely, checked the manuscript several times, and made many good suggestions.
Any flaws still in are my own responsibility.

And many thanks to Debbie McCormack, Belfast,
for the photos and artwork.

Published by Old Turnpike Publishing Limited
©2011 Peter McCormack
All rights reserved.
ISBN 978-0-9569374-0-7

Designed by April Sky Design www.aprilsky.co.uk
Printed by GPS Colour Graphics Limited

CONTENTS

PART TWO

PREFACE

This is the story of one man's search for God. It is not just a memoir, but a spiritual journey. It begins in the context of one of the most extreme fundamentalist Christian sects of Plymouth Brethren, which came to be known as Exclusive Brethren. From quite early in its existence the Plymouth Brethren movement fragmented regularly as people disagreed over doctrines and personalities. This is also true of the Exclusive branch, to the extent that it is difficult to define any one sect as the "original". The one described here is the loudest in its claims to be the pure line, but it has had schisms on a regular basis over the years. This is not intended as a condemnation of that sect; many, if not most, of its members are perfectly happy there and they have the right to live as they please. It is just not possible, however, to tell this story without including how his spiritual journey began there, and how he spent the first thirty-three years of his life in it before leaving it and being ostracised by his former friends and relations. The events described are from his memory of those years and are as accurate as human memory allows. Many people still in the sect will no doubt disagree as to what actually happened at certain times, and will most certainly put other interpretations on some of the events. As the story unfolds it will become clear that he is no longer claiming to have been a victim in any way, and holds no grudge against his former friends. He now knows it was just a part of his spiritual journey, and of theirs, but it has taken many years to arrive at that.

It is interwoven with a love affair that was severely tested by his and her search for meaning beyond the dogma, and by the search for freedom from the control of self-appointed Representatives of God on Earth. Peter's journey begins with his own early fanatical devotion to the sect, for which he takes full responsibility, and takes him through growing doubts, to the eventual total disillusionment with it, and the resulting ostracization from it. His life is so intertwined with that of Rachel, whose journey is in some ways in the opposite direction, that it is best told with her alongside. Because of the rigid structure of brethren beliefs, this journey involved traumatic choices for both of them. Despite their opposing beliefs they truly loved each other and their marriage survived the storms, until sadly ending with Rachel's early death.

Peter explores paths that take him completely away from Christianity and all religion, to years of agnosticism, and finally on to an intensive search for spiritual meaning. He combines his research into psychic mediums, near-death-experiences, hypnotic regressions, out-of-body projections, and the teachings of Ramtha and Seth, to form conclusions about the nature of God and the universe, and about the purpose of earth life.

Part one is told in the third person in order to set the context of his early life. In part two he takes over the story of his search for God from a personal point of view. In earlier years he was judgmental, and it may appear in parts of the story that he is still like that, because it took a long time to change, but by the end of the book it will be apparent that he no longer condemns anyone.

GLOSSARY OF BRETHREN LANGUAGE

Address: a speech to members only.

Assembly: word used for the church or the congregation, as in "going before the assembly".

Assembly Discipline: another term for withdrawing from. "he is under assembly discipline."

Brothers: the everyday word for men who are members.

Causing concern: stepping out of line.

Defect: someone who had been guilty of adultery or business failure, though forgiven, had a "defect" which meant certain limitations [from Leviticus 21 v 18].

Government of God: sinister term for something that might happen to you as retribution for sin, maybe taking ill or breaking a leg etc. Also connected with the "Defect", you are limited by the government of God.

Great Men of the Recovery: the brethren world leaders from Darby on, or "these great men".

Man of God: the world leader.

Meeting room: the church building.

Ministry: brethren literature.

Our Paul: common name for the Man of God [successor to Apostle Paul].

Out: as a noun, a person who has been withdrawn from, out of fellowship, as in excommunicated.

Position: the Position is the common name for the brethren fellowship; "the Lord is with the position" was a common mantra.

Preaching:	an address specifically on the Gospel, the one meeting which could include strangers in the audience.
Reading meeting:	conversational meeting, bible reading.
Saints:	brethren regularly refer to themselves as "the saints"; all other institutions of government or transport etc are solely there to serve the saints.
Self-judgment:	constant soul searching.
Shut up:	to be shut up is to be temporarily isolated from all contact until the elders deem you fit for fellowship again [from Leviticus 13 v50].
Sisters:	the everyday word for women who are members.
Subject:	required behaviour of a wife towards her husband.
Three-day-meetings:	their word for conference.
Universal Position:	the worldwide membership of the fellowship.
Withdrawn from:	excommunicated and ostracized.
Worldly:	as a noun this refers to everybody outside of the brethren, as in "he is a worldly".

CHAPTER 1
Peter, the early years.

Peter, now in his sixtieth year, was reflecting on the course of his life. Physically he was healthy. Mentally he was now quite calm and composed, but this had certainly not always been the case. Spiritually, he was unrecognisable from his beginnings in the Christian sect into which he had been born.

What a spiritual journey his life had been, he reflected. His parents had been members of one of the strictest branches of the Plymouth Brethren, that had been started by J N Darby in 1832 in Plymouth, England. It became known as Exclusive Brethren. 'Separation from evil' was the basis of its beliefs. The whole system was built on one single verse of scripture in 2 Timothy 2, verse 19, "Let him that names the name of the Lord withdraw from iniquity". It was taken out of context to stand alone as an absolute truth in itself, taking precedence over every other verse of scripture. As time went by the word iniquity was defined in increasingly narrow terms by Darby and the leaders who succeeded him. Darby claimed to have had a vision in which he saw his mission was to recover "the faith once delivered to the saints" [Jude 3:1]. He travelled widely and found thousands of people willing to follow his teachings, establishing churches, or 'meetings' in brethren terminology, throughout Britain and Ireland, Europe, North and South America, Australia and New Zealand, and the odd outpost in eastern lands. There are particular times in history when new religions are born or new versions of Christianity created. Powerful personalities can always find followers, and Darby was a strong character, hugely egotistical, focused and demanding. He was intellectual, combative, and convinced of his own infallibility. He came up with a new translation of the bible, and wrote many books condemning the established Church. Anyone in the movement who disagreed with him was pushed out, or "withdrawn from", a phrase that would later come to strike terror into members everywhere because of its devastating effect on families.

Peter's parents were married in 1944. His father George was 30 and his mother Maureen was 19, and with hindsight the marriage was perhaps too impulsive. It was maybe a great ego boost for George to attract a teenage bride, but his teenage bride was unfortunately very naive and starry-eyed, and the marriage soon began to wobble. Their first child was Irene in 1945, followed by Alan in 1947. Tragedy struck in September 1949 when after a pleasant family weekend of blackberry-picking, Irene took ill with what turned out to be a very virulent form of diphtheria. Within a week, only four years old, she had passed away. As is often the case, such a tragedy put an enormous strain on their marriage, and they said things to each other that could never be mended. He accused her of having idolized Irene to the extreme that God had stepped in and taken her, which was an absurd statement. She accused him of caring more about religion than about anything else, which had some truth in it. They still had some good times, and it must have taken enormous courage to just carry on with life, but the marriage was very unstable and suffered from many temper tantrums on both sides. Peter was born the following August, 1950. Another girl, Marjorie, completed the family in 1952. George had been brought up in an assembly of Plymouth Brethren, but moved to the Exclusive Brethren in his early twenties, along with one of his closest friends. His move caused considerable distress to his family of four sisters and four brothers and his parents, but he had become fascinated by the Exclusive teachings. Maureen was only three when her parents had made a similar move, though they came from a more traditional background of the established Church. There was a period of time in the 1930s when many people seemed to be newly attracted to the EB for some reason, but this slowed down, and in more modern times virtually no one who is not born to it ever joins it.

In 1953 Peter was taken to hospital with Scarlet Fever. This was considered more serious then than now, and the symptoms were scarily similar to the diphtheria that had taken Irene, which really terrified his parents. He never forgot being carried out in the dead of night to a waiting cream-coloured ambulance, its engine purring softly, and a blue light at the rear. He was kept in isolation for two weeks and couldn't understand why his parents could only wave at him from outside a window. He received loads of toys and teddy bears, but he wanted his family. And every day the nurses held him down in order to give him injections in his thigh. He resisted them fiercely and loudly every time. When he got home he was unable to stand, possibly because of being bedridden for two weeks. It was odd, standing up as usual every time and promptly falling over, but it caused great amusement all round and he was soon better.

There was no Sunday School for children. They were taken to the meetings along with the adults and were expected to sit silently and listen to whatever they could understand. No one really made any effort to find out if they understood what was going on, and as long as they were well-behaved it was fine. It was left to their parents to worry about their children growing up, hopefully taking their rightful place in the fellowship, or alternatively to face the nightmare of their children turning away and rejecting the Truth. Naturally, many children just daydreamed to get away from the boredom. Peter had done his share of daydreaming, but he was a serious child and he sometimes found it interesting. He never doubted the constant assertions that the Brethren were God's special people, the Saints, the people who knew the Truth better than anyone in any other church, the people who had the most Light. He was 9 years old when a new world leader emerged and began a revival that would become more and more extreme over the next 50 years. He introduced a new rule forcing all brethren children to opt out of Religious Instruction and assembly at school. It meant having to sit out separate from friends with his younger sister in a waiting room until it was alright to return to class. The room had a gas fire, and he and his sister would huddle together in front of it during the winter months. He and his sister were best friends, and being together in this was a great help. School sports and all extra-curricular activities were also now forbidden. All members including children could no longer socialise with any non-member, to the extent that you couldn't eat your lunch alongside your friends. Non-members were defined as worldly people, or "worldlies". The only person worse than a worldly one was an "Out"--this was anyone who had been withdrawn from, an out-of-fellowship person. You could speak to worldly people, but you would not have any contact whatsoever with an "Out"--no matter how well you had known them or even if they were closely related to you. Peter would wonder sometimes what it was like to be out of fellowship, away from God, under the power of the Devil, and he would shiver inside. Whenever he would see such a person on the street he would look at them with a kind of awe in the way that people stare at road accidents.

At the age of nine therefore Peter's world was narrowing ever further from ordinary gospel-hall strictness to being virtually cut off from the usual world that most people experienced. Over the years the world leader, now known as the Man of God, [MOG for short] issued a constant stream of new rules called directives, which applied to almost every aspect of daily life, controlling where you lived, how you dressed, how you styled your hair, who you married, where you could and could not work, and a thousand other details. It had always been forbidden to have or to listen to the radio, to have or to watch TV, to go to the cinema or theatre, or to eat at restaurants, and now it was wrong to read novels or religious books that were not brethren approved. University education was forbidden, and you could not be in a professional or trade association. Brethren ignored the celebration of Christmas and Easter, although many parents cheated a little and bought presents for their children coincidently close to December 25. When computers came on the scene they were banned as well, as were mobile phones. Even automatic garage door openers and remote control devices for the ill or elderly were prohibited on the basis that they had radio components. Radio was linked to "the prince of the power of the air, the spirit that now works in the children of disobedience" [Ephesians 2 v2]. For their own convenience however they managed to overlook the radio problem when it came to flying in aeroplanes. The airline owned the plane so it was not the brethren's responsibility.

There was a meeting every weeknight, Saturday morning, Sunday at 6am and all day. Life was centred around the fellowship, and you had to explain yourself if you were absent from a meeting. Smoking was forbidden, but for reasons we will see later it became fine to drink alcohol. The effect of being cut off like this from the world outside was to focus all attention inwards on the closed world of meetings, and as a result a unique way of life was created. To this day ex-members from any part of the world have a unique bond if they happen to meet, an understanding that few others can share fully. Individual thinking was stamped upon. The Truth was absolute and was defined by the Man of God. If the Man of God changed his mind that was because "the Lord was moving on". To question the authority of the leader was to invite instant expulsion. Along with most members Peter soon became stunted in his outlook, believing that the world was wicked and dangerous and that sin was to be feared and guarded against at every moment. His own introspective nature absorbed the fear like a sponge.

At school around this time, in the last year of Primary School, or what would be called Year 7 in some cultures, his teacher was also a member of Plymouth Brethren, although not Exclusive. He was, however, a Puritan in the same mould as the leaders Peter was used to. He would often sentimentally say that the reason he had wanted to become a teacher was so that he could tell little boys and girls about Jesus. An hour later he would be in a rage about something and physically beating up some unfortunate child. Sometimes the child's screams would bring the lady teacher from the next classroom to the rescue. Once he hit Peter on the head with his pen, which flew into pieces. While he raged about how hard Peter's head must be, Peter was trying rather unsuccessfully to suppress a fit of giggles, and this made him even angrier. If you got less than six out of ten in spellings you were caned. Since you swopped your book with your neighbour in order to mark them as the teacher called out the answers, it became a matter of compassion to make sure your neighbour didn't get less than six. However this practice was eventually exposed and the teacher went into another righteous rage, fulminating about all the lying and cheating. Knowing Peter's background he singled him out for extra punishment and laid huge guilt on him. He made him write out a hundred times: "Against thee, thee only, have I sinned, and done this evil in thy sight", quoting the lament of King David in Psalm 51, when he had been rebuked for causing the death of one of his soldiers so that he could have his wife Bathsheba. Peter was ten years old, and wasn't at all sure that his own crime was quite as bad as that, but apparently one sin was as bad as another. He had to take a note home to his parents and they were just as horrified as the teacher at such evil behaviour.

One Sunday morning an old man died in the Breaking of Bread meeting. He had just been standing at the table to "gave thanks for the loaf" and slowly collapsed as he went back to his seat. He was laid out on a wooden form while a doctor was fetched, and just once made a last feeble effort to get up before expiring. Nobody else moved for an hour until at last the medics came, with a policeman, and the body was carried out. Peter was terrified, and had nightmares for weeks afterwards. The policeman apparently remarked on the great quiet dignity that was shown by the brethren, especially the children. As soon as the body was removed they then resumed the service and completed it as normal. That was what brethren did; there would be no drama or histrionics just because someone had collapsed and died. Peter never forgot that. About six years later another man took ill and died quite noisily during a conference, which the brethren called a 3-day meeting. On that occasion the proceedings were not even paused; he was carried out to die in the foyer, and the rest of the brethren were told to keep their attention on the speaker. Peter was learning that God was indeed a harsh God.

Many times as a child he secretly resented the duty to go to the meeting. In the early days when you were still allowed to go to the beach in the summer holidays you had to come home early to get ready for the meeting. At school when you had loads of homework to do you had to do it before or after the meeting. Meetings, meetings, meetings, discussing dry doctrines from a passage of scripture, or else getting at someone who was causing concern. It seemed to Peter that the flow of negative criticism was endless, but some of that was undoubtedly due to his own introverted nature. You were a sinner, and even when you repented you still had more sinfulness underneath. The one thing he did enjoy was the silence before the meeting started, as people came in and took their seats. The old hall had a bare wooden floor, with a strip of brown linoleum up the aisle, pockmarked by the ladies' stiletto heels. The seats were plain wooden forms or benches, also brown. The heating system consisted of ancient large diameter pipes, also brown, which gurgled and murmured a language of their own, and you could somehow smell the heat as well as feel its warmth. Peter knew it was powered by an ancient coke-burning boiler in a dusty cellar that you reached by way of a steel ladder. He often accompanied his father down there to light it and keep it stoked up. In that period before the meeting started he would sit and soak up the atmosphere; it was so tranquil and relaxed; a few people might whisper to each other; someone would cough; the pipes would make their own sounds; a lady's perfume might waft across his nostrils; there was the rustle of skirts, footstools being positioned with a scraping sound; somehow the whole scene soothed his mind and he felt a strange pleasant tingling in his head.

His parents were kind and devoted to their children. They were both good people, but would have been even better people if they had stayed away from each other. His father was fascinated by the brethren literature, the "ministry", and he spent hours reading and rereading it, and he could quote reams of it at the drop of a hat. He would never miss a meeting and was always travelling to nearby meetings at weekends wherever there was one. His mother didn't read the ministry and preferred to skip as many meetings as possible, using the children as an excuse. There was a bit of a crisis when Peter, about twelve by now, began suffering from a kind of vertigo. This came on him mostly during meetings; as he sat in his chair the whole room seemed to be tilting around him, and it was quite frightening. It happened very occasionally at school, but most of the time it was in the meeting rooms. The cause was never really established and he was treated with herbal medicines without much improvement. The worst part was that his father was convinced that he was putting it on because he didn't want to go to the meetings, thus piling on some more guilt. With hindsight, it was most probably a nervous reaction to the deep fear and guilt that Peter seemed to absorb all the time. He really did believe in the great struggle and conflict that raged between God and the Devil, with one of the battlefields being his own soul. With further hindsight in later years he wondered at the effect of being born so soon after the tragic death of his sister; did he absorb the fear and sorrow before he was even born?

He moved into his teenage years never imagining that he had any other options but to live a lifetime in the brethren movement. There were teenagers who rebelled and rejected it all. They would be withdrawn from and their parents would be brokenhearted and devastated, having to eject their son or daughter from the home and never contact them again. Peter loved his family life and it was too much to even consider breaking it up. At eighteen he fell in love with a girl at work, a 'worldly' girl, and he came close to leaving the fellowship for her. Yet in the end he just couldn't do it. Only those who have experienced that kind of brainwashing in a cult would understand the power of it over the individual.

For him to continue having some enjoyment in life all doubts would have to be suppressed. Emotions were suppressed. Sexual desires were repressed and feared. God was to be feared; God was loving only if you did what he said, otherwise he got really angry. He watched over you all day and night and noted down your sinful thoughts and deeds. Peter became ever more conscious of that harsh God following his every move. He had been born with Original Sin and only by fighting his evil nature would he ever reach peace with God. In his teens now, the lust he felt for pretty girls was so powerful that he shook sometimes, and he knew it was the work of the devil in him. Entertaining very sinful thoughts was always followed by remorse and self-loathing and bewilderment. He would silently confess his sin to the angry God and beg for forgiveness, only to sin again and again in the same way. He wondered if he might be actually possessed by the devil. He read his bible every day, even taking it to school with him, hoping to find a way out of his sinfulness.

He spent five years at Secondary School, and his talents began to blossom considerably. It was an experimental school and many of the teachers were really gifted and approachable. They were not afraid to lark around with the boys, and they created a really relaxed atmosphere in which to learn. One year he came top of the class in every subject except one, which was geography for some reason. In spite of his religious drawbacks he made many good friends, with boys from all walks of life and with many of the teachers. It was an all-boys school unfortunately, but the girls' school was nearby. His English teacher was also responsible for Religious Instruction, and he soon got around the matter of Peter having to leave the room by seamlessly merging the English class with the RI, or RE as it later became. Thus the class became a lively debating forum, with Peter defending his beliefs quite competently, and often humorously. He gained respect for his integrity and his lack of pomposity. The EB had no organ or any musical accompaniment in their meetings, and one day in class Peter was stoutly defending this practice; as he spoke, however, he couldn't help hearing the dirge-like singing in his head and he laughingly conceded defeat. The teacher himself was agnostic and would often corner Peter as school ended and debate with him for hours. Those five years of his life provided him above all with the ability to think for himself, which was to become very important as time went on. The EB rules forbade university education, as they suspected, rightly, that young minds would become open to wider philosophies, or in their words, corrupted by worldly thinking. So, sadly, this blossoming of his talents was cut short, and he left school at seventeen. He lost contact with every single one of those friends as he disappeared completely into the exclusive fellowship once more.

He was a keen reader at home and like his father he began to read the 'Ministry', as the brethren books were called. These were the books written by Darby, and hundreds of books of recorded meetings of ministry given by the leaders who followed Darby, the Great Men of the Recovery, as they were referred to. Peter absorbed the teachings and was soon able to preach and give addresses at the meetings himself while still in his teens. He became one of the fanatical 'committed young men' who would assure the future of the brethren movement, and was accepted into the inner circle of those who knew everything that went on at the top. He even spent an afternoon with the world leader, the Man of God himself, and this added to his own authority. He became more and more absorbed in the culture of his strange closed world. With hindsight, he could see that he had often had many doubts, but they were quickly repressed. Besides, it was quite a nice boost to his ego to be looked up to as a talented speaker and potential future leader.

He got a job as a trainee production manager in a printing firm and studied for the exams, once again getting top grades. Yet the job was unfulfilling and he felt restless and frustrated. The factory was full of pretty girls and the opportunities were limitless, yet always, no matter how close he got to them, he would mysteriously pull back. They would be hurt and puzzled, and he couldn't explain to them what was really at the root of it. How could you explain that you couldn't even take a girl to the cinema, because [a] it was wrong, and [b] you had to go to a meeting instead? How did you chat to a girl about last night's TV when you hadn't the slightest idea of what she was on about? How did you talk about the news when you never actually caught up with it until you saw the local evening paper?

Seeking to better himself he moved to the Civil Service and began studying for promotion there. But though he took the exams with his customary ease, and accumulated qualifications, he soon found that the Civil Service had about three times as many staff as it really needed. All the qualifications in the world were not going to move him through the crowds of people in front of him. The one thing that might help would be social networking, getting in with the right people, but for an EB member that was impossible. He couldn't even go out for a quick drink with workmates after work, never mind make serious friends. No doubt many other brethren were going through similar frustrations but it was never talked about. From a historical distance the answers seem obvious, but at the time it was just like being a spider in a jar; you tried this way and that way and nothing worked.

His brother was self-employed, selling clothing to retailers on commission, and after another couple of years Peter left the Civil Service and joined him. Although he loved the freedom of being self-employed, however, he did not enjoy being a salesman, and so career success continued to elude him. For a while he did a self-employed delivery service, driving a van every day, which he quite enjoyed. Eventually both brothers joined their father in starting a business together in locks, keys and hardware. The truth was his talents lay elsewhere and by not listening to his inner voice he continued to be frustrated.

CHAPTER 2
Rachel, the early years

Five hundred miles away on the south coast of England Rachel was born in 1952, also into that same Exclusive Brethren sect. Her parents had lost twin babies at birth a couple of years previously, and Rachel would be an only child. She was a shy sweet-tempered girl and her parents doted on her. The world of this EB is the same everywhere, being closely monitored by its leaders from the top down, so Rachel grew up with the same set of rules in the same narrow-minded little society. She was fortunate to have a group of brethren friends of the same age who attended the same schools as she did and thus it was easier to be separate from the worldly people without being too isolated. It was not in Rachel's nature to question any of the rules. It was not that she really accepted the rules as such, she just didn't think about them at all. She had enough friends around her to keep her happy and therefore felt no sense of being deprived. Not once did she ever think that life could be different. Life was just the way it was and she had no complaints. It was a positive attribute, this inner contentment, but such a temperament was open to being abused by the leaders who sought to control people.

In the meetings she simply daydreamed, or carried on whispered conversations with friends, blissfully unaware of the disapproving stares of pious ladies nearby. All of the serious discussions, whether it was preaching hellfire or outlining doctrinal stuff, or the more common 'getting at' somebody who was less than committed, whatever it was, just passed her by. She didn't deliberately not listen; she just never thought of it. She was vaguely aware of the warnings about sin and worldliness, but she viewed all that stuff as something for the future when she would grow up and maybe get married. Unlike Peter, no thought of being a guilty sinner ever really crossed her mind.

She grew into teenage years like this, blossoming into a stunningly beautiful girl, with rich thick dark hair worn loose around her beautiful face. She had big brown eyes, smooth skin, and sensuous lips. Only her roman nose seemed a little out of proportion, especially to catty women who envied her, but she was still utterly gorgeous to look at. She had great legs and a fabulous figure, shown off to full effect in the short skirts and dresses that were the fashion in the sixties. Her personality was bubbly and her smile was enchanting, and she laughed a lot. Although she had a kind of innocence about her it was impossible for her not to notice the effect she had on men, both young and old. Besides that, she found she was just as fascinated by men as they were by her. Though still not given to introspection she did sometimes wonder why some of the leaders who would fulminate against short skirts in the meeting would also look longingly at her thighs every chance they got.

Unlike Peter, she never spent any time worrying about her sexual desires. She and her best friend were normal teenage girls, boy-mad, and with no religious hang-ups to hold them back. She still tended to drift through life without taking any serious thought about it. Settling down and being good was still something for the future. Fortunately the leaders in her meeting were less vigilant than in most places and neither she nor her friend were ever caught out breaking the rules. She hung out with the least-committed young guys who knew how to have fun, and she and her friend would often mock the serious boys who resembled the still unknown Peter far away in Belfast. She went to the cinema, drank in pubs, went to parties, and did everything a healthy teenager would do. Yet around the meetings she still retained that sweet air of innocence and older men and women liked her and enjoyed her exuberant sense of fun. Though not seriously minded, she was no airhead; underneath that lighthearted and bubbly nature was a deeply caring, gentle and very intelligent character. It would be fair to say that she was to prove in many respects to be personally far above the narrow thinking of religious fanaticism, even if, paradoxically, she failed to detect anything wrong with the brethren system.

She left school to attend business college, and became proficient in secretarial skills like shorthand and typing. Her best friend attended the same college, training to be a dental nurse, and so they always had each other for company. They travelled to a nearby city for college, but there were brethren nearby and they would go there for lunch. This was one of the ways that brethren sought to protect their young people from getting into "sin", and on the surface it was pleasant enough. Rachel and her friend always found ways round it when they wanted to meet up with other friends. Despite the close watch of the brethren and the need for confessing to wrongdoing from time to time, Rachel never lifted the veil on her life at this time, beyond broad hints, and of course she was right. She went to work in an insurance office, and after less than a year transferred to a brethren builders' firm, acting as secretary to the directors, one of whom fell in love with her, although he was already married, and nothing was to come of it.

CHAPTER 3
The Man of God

The current Man of God, the son of the previous one who had reigned over the brethren for fifty years, was the one who had seized the leadership in 1959 with his abrupt challenge to the brethren to become ever more separate from the world. Many of them split away at this time, creating yet another schism to add to the long history of schisms in brethren history. They were not prepared to give up contact with their relatives and friends who were non-brethren. Families were divided, couples broken up, and many lives were blighted. Yet the Leader retained the support of the majority and went on to issue his non-stop directives for the next eleven years until his death in 1970. He lived in Brooklyn, New York, and spoke with a harsh New York accent. He was fond of whiskey, as his father had been before him, and he appeared to drink quite heavily. It was rumoured that an illness which laid him up in hospital in the mid-sixties was actually an attempt to conquer alcoholism, but this was and still is fiercely denied in the EB. A Man of God, God's own Representative on Earth, would not be subject to such weakness.

However, he drank openly, and since the brethren, like many Christians then and now, were mostly against alcohol, it was becoming a subject creating unrest. He hit on the ingenious solution of making alcohol virtually compulsory for everyone. He promoted a doctrine that alcohol was one of God's creatures and therefore it was wrong to forbid it. Prohibition became a 'test of fellowship'. In brethren terms a test of fellowship was a principle that you had to accept if you wished to remain as a member. The principle was established that prohibition of alcohol was against the Man of God. The result was that alcohol became a prominent feature of brethren life. If someone visited your home the first thing you did was serve them alcohol, because at the very least not to do so would make you suspect. Peter was fifteen when he was introduced to whiskey.

It is impossible to say how many alcoholics or heavy drinkers were created as a result of this manoeuvre, but drink became very prevalent. Possibly it went a long way to relieving the underlying tedium of brethren life, though no one would admit to any such thing. Ironically it led to the spectacular downfall of the revered Man of God. In 1970 while on a tour of the UK he began to fondle many of the young women while he sat drinking in the homes of various brethren. He would pull them on to his knee and fondle their breasts, sometimes in a room full of people and at other times late at night in the garden. Many were teenagers and too scared and bewildered to protest. Some were married women whose husbands had to sit and watch. Most of these women were very unworldly and chaste, and the experience was deeply traumatising for them. By today's standards at least, the actions were criminal. On the final weekend of his tour, in Aberdeen, Scotland, he was found in bed with the willing naked wife of another brother. He said she was acting as his nurse, though it could be argued that not many nurses strip off in the course of their duties. Her husband was also a willing participant in this arrangement, of course, believing it a privilege to lend his wife to such an august man. The Leader had also disgraced himself that same day with a drunken performance in public at one of his meetings, using inappropriate language and sexual innuendo. On that night that he was discovered in bed with his 'nurse' by two or three concerned brothers, a doctor was called and he diagnosed alcoholic dementia, but this was later strongly rejected by his supporters. He was spirited away, back to New York, before the weekend was complete. Once again, however, the brethren movement was convulsed and many thousands split away to form an even greater variety of independent brethren fellowships. It became known as the Aberdeen Matter. He quickly recovered his aplomb and managed to bluff his way through, by saying that God had told him to do what he did, and amazingly managed to retain most of his followers. People who knew the true facts of what had gone on were ruthlessly silenced by being withdrawn from, often on his say-so alone, sometimes even by phone before they could reach home. This was against all the established procedures in the local meetings, but such was his power that he got away with it. He even smeared a very prominent and well-loved leading brother, who had been one of the people who had discovered him in the bed, by alleging quite falsely that he was homosexual. He kept control therefore but died a few months later. It has to be said that the legend among the EB to this very day is that he was a Pure Man and was at all times acting under God's instructions. This is presumably possible, though certainly rejected by those who split away. God moves in mysterious ways. Peter certainly believed it for quite a number of years.

CHAPTER 4
Peter and Rachel

Still unaware of each other's existence, both Peter and Rachel were among those who stayed loyal to this Leader in 1970, and so remained in the same fellowship. It is difficult to describe the hold that such a system has over normally intelligent people. In ten years a new myth had grown very powerful, that the leaders of the EB, that is, the pure line from Darby onwards, were the direct spiritual descendants of the apostle Paul. The Truth of Christianity had somehow stumbled along and survived in a muddled way through the ages since Paul's time, and then Darby had taken up the baton in the nineteenth century. Darby and his successors were Apostles in the same mould as Paul. It was a bold claim, quite without any basis whatever in scripture or anywhere else, yet Peter remembered being quite taken with the idea. An Apostle like the current Man of God therefore could not fail; it was inconceivable. It was this that convinced him more than anything else that the Aberdeen Matter had not been a failure of holiness on the MOG's part.

A new 'apostle' took over the world leadership when this one died. He was a dour man, even stricter than his predecessors and power-mad. He drank whiskey too, of course, but where drink had made the former MOG sometimes merry and witty and entertaining in his own way, it made the new leader angry and sullen and hypercritical. There had been two other candidates for the position, though nothing was ever official in the EB. One was the son of the previous leader and another was an African American from Barbados. It just sort of drifted for a while until the winner got the upper hand with his superior political skills. Nobody was ever elected to office in the EB; democracy was despised, and indeed the brethren did not vote in government elections either. He set about purging all the local leaders who had been favourites of his predecessor, and set himself up as an absolute monarch. Like one of the biblical kings, "whom he would he slew, and whom he would he kept alive", metaphorically speaking. On a memorable occasion at which Peter was present, and sitting close enough to hear, this MOG spoke across to a local leader after a meeting had just finished and the sound system was off. He said, "You don't like me Mr B. do you?" The man replied that he did indeed like the MOG, he had no problem with him. This was sufficient for the man to be "withdrawn from" the next night for "disagreeing with the Man of God". Obviously, if he had agreed with the MOG he would still have met the same fate, only "for not liking the MOG"!

He appointed his own favourites everywhere and the ordinary rank-and-file of brethren became even more tightly controlled than before. Eventually under his rule travel was only allowed if you asked permission, and if you didn't get permission you didn't travel. Similarly you eventually had to ask for specific approval to marry someone and if the answer was no you had to look for another. Oddly enough many of the favourites he promoted turned out to be disappointments who let him down. In some cases they didn't do anything obvious to let him down but he would simply turn against them for no apparent reason. Then they would be humiliated and sometimes withdrawn from. This happened so often that Peter couldn't help doubting this MOG's judgment. On one occasion he turned against a man he had promoted and it resulted in great tragedy: while shut up, the man axed his wife and children to death and then hanged himself. The MOG said this was the work of the Devil. He promoted one particular man, named Henry, above all others as his second-in-command, and he lauded him as a very spiritual man. Many of these plaudits were recorded in meetings that were later printed as part of the 'Ministry'. However, Henry the great favourite fell spectacularly from grace when a local sister confessed to having an affair with him. The MOG then said that he had always suspected the man was too good to be true. This comment was also printed up in the Ministry, yet no one would dare point out that it was a brazen lie contradicting the earlier assertions.

That was still in the future though in 1971. The brethren tradition was to hold conferences, called 3-day meetings, in most of the cities that had fairly large numbers. Visitors from around the world attended by invitation and would be accommodated in the homes of the local brethren. It became customary for young single sisters to go as helpers, that is, to stay in the home to prepare meals and help out with the chores whilst the owners would attend the meetings. Rachel and a friend went to a certain home at the 3-day meetings in the city of Dublin in 1971. Peter was one of the guests staying in the house to which she went.

For the rest of his life Peter would remember with vivid clarity the moment Rachel came through the front door of that house in Dublin. He was mesmerised. She wore a simple short figure-hugging dress; her long lustrous dark hair framed her lovely face; as she entered she was talking and laughing. She caught his look and smiled at him and went on upstairs. From that moment until now she had never been out of his thoughts for more than a minute. He paid her a lot of attention, and he had to ask the owner of the house for permission to take her out for a walk in the evening. The man thought it over and then granted permission, stipulating that they should be back by ten o'clock! With official permission granted, he asked Rachel if she would come out with him and she quickly said yes. He noticed that she didn't ask about any permission being needed. They tried to leave by the back door but found the outer gate locked, and had to come back in and scuttle past the room full of brethren guests. As they walked together Peter found himself utterly charmed not only by her physical beauty but by an indefinable quality about her that was a mixture of gentleness and fun, with an understated intelligence. She was not intellectual and she obviously had no grasp of EB doctrines and rules, but in an odd way this made her even more attractive to the somewhat staid and serious Peter. For her part Rachel liked him a lot, and even went north to visit his home in Belfast for a couple of days. Before she had set out her boss and her parents had warned her on no account to go to Belfast because of the riots and bombs. She didn't seem to feel as passionately about him as he felt about her, but to venture into riot-torn Belfast to see more of him must have meant something. She was put off by his seriousness and his image as the type of 'committed young brother' that she would often mock at home in her own meeting. Peer pressure probably reinforced this. Yet in a way she was puzzled about why she liked him at all. All her boyfriends had been rule-breakers, the kind of 'bad' guys who always attracted the girls. Peter was the kind of guy she would normally giggle about with her best friend. Yet she perceived another side to him underneath the staid image. He had a self-mocking humour and he had a way of making clever little quips about life in general that surprised her in that they amused her so deeply, often making her smile a long time afterwards. When she returned to England he lingered in her thoughts more than she wanted him to, but in a characteristic way of hers, which we will see more of, she let the thoughts remain neutral.

Nevertheless, he pursued her with relentless passion. They lived a long way apart so it was difficult to get to see her. In those days hopping on a plane was relatively more expensive than it is now, and anyway it all had to be done within the limited world of the EB. People also forget what it was like to use the telephone in those days; you still had to go through the operator, often waiting for up to an hour before one replied to you. He tried to arrange to meet her at a three-day meeting in England being chaired by the MOG himself, but Rachel said the MOG was boring and she didn't fancy sitting through his long dreary meetings! This should have put him off her, but it didn't. So when he did eventually manage to see her he felt under enormous pressure to make the time count. Unfortunately this made him seem too intense, which he already was anyway, and Rachel would be left feeling that he was putting her under intolerable pressure. At one point she agreed to get engaged to him, but a month later she changed her mind. She really didn't want to get married at all to anyone at this stage. She was possibly torn between the opinions of her closest friends and by her own deeper instincts. It was also part of her character to draw back from serious decision making. She visited him in Belfast for the last time to tell him that there was no future in their relationship. Peter was extremely disappointed and depressed. Affairs like this were always conducted in the glare of brethren attention, which was really quite immature at times, and this was an added sort of humiliation. For so-called saints the brethren could often be really cruel, and Peter's failure to get his girl was a great source of fun, with much sniggering and childish spite.

A few days after she went home he wrote a last letter to her:

> *Dear Rachel,*
>
> *I was very disappointed in your decision to end our relationship, as you know, but I appreciate your honesty. You can't make yourself have feelings you don't have. I think I will always remember you, even though I will try very hard to forget. Nobody else ever had such an effect on me, and I can't seem to change that feeling, but that's my problem not yours.*
> *I assure you this is the last you will hear from me, which is what you want. I just want to wish you well in whatever you do in your life. The man you eventually choose, if you do, will be a lucky man.*
>
> *Peter*

The only reason for recording this is that, not for the first or the last time in his life, Peter had a deep instinctive feeling that there was more to come, though still very ignorant of where that feeling came from. Eventually over many years he came to recognise an inner self that knows more than the intellect. He suspected it wasn't the end of the affair, but at the same time he had absolutely no logical reason for thinking this, and so he began the painful process of trying to forget about her. At least he had the advantage of not seeing her.

He was surprised then about a month later when she phoned him. Rachel had been quite deeply affected by his brief letter, and try as she might, she couldn't put it out of her mind. He wrote good letters, as she knew; she had always particularly enjoyed his letters to her. The final brief letter should have rounded off the whole experience on a good note; he had expressed no hard feelings, and he had kept his word and left her alone. Yet something kept niggling at her. There was something endearing about his last letter that she couldn't explain. There was something endearing about Peter that she couldn't explain. One day as she sat with her bed-ridden grandmother the conversation turned to what her grandmother called her Irish boy. Rachel told her it was finished, and tried to laugh it off. Her grandmother could barely see at this stage, but she suddenly straightened up with great effort and looked straight at her in a way she would never forget and said, "Be sensible, Rachel". That was all she said, but it had a powerful effect. So after a few days of turmoil she phoned Peter and explained rather hesitatingly that she would like to see him again.

Peter of course was torn about how to respond. He was just about managing to begin the process of getting over her and he didn't want to get drawn in again only to be disappointed. However he did agree to meet her and he travelled to England to see her. He stayed in London at a brethren house for a few days and then drove down to Hampshire to meet her at a railway station a few miles north of where she lived. Due to some recent glorious weather he was tanned and looking his best. Rachel remembered years later that her heart missed a beat when she saw him again, though Peter was totally unaware of the effect he was having. They spent what turned out to be a magical day together in Hampshire and London. On the way up to London they stopped to visit a bird sanctuary. Peter was nervous and awkward, anxious not to take anything for granted, so he didn't touch her. They walked round the sanctuary for a while, a distinct distance between them, and suddenly Rachel thrust her arm into his. She always remembered ever after his enthusiastic response to that gesture. The ice was broken. From then on he was relaxed and amusing, and she found herself being thoroughly charmed. They posed for a street photo outside the Planetarium that Peter would treasure all his life, reminding him of how stunningly beautiful Rachel was. In the darkness of the Planetarium she returned his kiss with a passion that he would remember forever. When it was time to go home she accompanied him to Heathrow Airport, and a few minutes before his flight was due she told him she would rather he didn't leave. This was another of her characteristics that he would come to know so well, leaving everything to the last minute before deciding on things. However, it was clear that something good was happening and Peter agreed to stay at her house for the weekend. From then on the relationship slowly blossomed and they were married in the following spring, 1973. She really hadn't imagined that she would settle down in a serious relationship until some vague time well into the future. But she would later admit that a part of her 'knew' all along that he was the man for her. In the face of very testing experiences over many years they remained devoted to each other.

Following brethren custom, she gave up work and moved to live in Belfast to be a full-time housewife, subject to her husband. Unless there were very special circumstances brethren wives were not permitted to go out to work. In their world the man was regarded as the head of his wife and of the home, and this doctrine was accepted as natural law. Rachel changed from being rather flighty [in brethren terms] to being serious and 'good'. Her belief was that when you settled down you had to be mature and pious and leave all the days of freedom and fun behind, which, had she analysed it, would have explained why she resisted getting married in the first place. Ironically, just as she was turning away from freedom, Peter was beginning to taste and like some freedom. They lived out their brethren routine, and they were very much in love, and happy enough with life as it unfolded. They spent every possible moment together, as lovers, companions and best friends. A son was born a year after they were married, and daughters two years and a year again after that. Birth control was forbidden in the EB, but this was fortunately not strictly enforceable, even for the fanatics who were in control, though at least one woman was questioned closely when she ceased having children. People in a society full of oppressive rules and laws will always find themselves having to draw a line at times when constant obedience is demanded. Even so, the birth rate was higher by far than in a more liberal society.

In 1980, after an apparently normal full-term pregnancy, Rachel gave birth to a fourth child, a stillborn daughter. It was an emotional trauma for her, and although Peter was basically sympathetic his support for her was quite inadequate. The religious side of his nature was cold and hard, and he regarded a still birth as just a failed pregnancy, a biological event. On the advice of the brethren they purchased a grave and gave the child a proper burial. However, even the brethren were vague and non-committal about the status of a still-born child, and they did not hold a proper full funeral service in the meeting hall. A few hand-picked guests went to the cemetery and Peter alone spoke briefly, committing the body to God, the Artificer of Life. There were those, like Rachel's mother, who held the opinion that such a child would not be in heaven, having not been baptised. The EB official line continued to be vague about it all and they preferred to say as little as possible about it.

In the summertime they would go to Rachel's parents on the south coast of England for two or three weeks. Peter loved these trips with his wife and children, although his in-laws were not particularly friendly to him. Rachel's mother was quite eccentric and her religious beliefs were in some respects even more extreme than those of the official EB culture. As a child Rachel was forbidden to wear red shoes, for instance. Her mother held many Victorian beliefs about sexuality and class. Sexual intercourse was solely for the purpose of reproduction, and not to be indulged in for any other reason. When Rachel's fifth child was born it was decided she should be called Diana, and her mother moved heaven and earth to try and stop this, even sending over two of her aunts to intervene. Diana is the name of a goddess and therefore it would be idolatry to name a child like that. Peter registered the name before the aunts arrived and they were too late to do anything about it. He couldn't help pointing out to them that Rachel's mother's sister was called Mary, and a certain Mary in history had more than her fair share of worshippers. Her father was also semi-detached from what passed for normal life even in the brethren, and was convinced that there was no good purpose to being in this world; the only purpose was to deny the comforts of the flesh and look forward to the "world to come". Ordinary natural pleasure, or "gratification of the flesh" was to be shunned as much as possible. This made it quite difficult for Peter to relate to them, and they did not make much attempt to get to know him. However, since most brethren at this period were forbidden to travel unless on business, it was a bonus to have relatives in a seaside town. Readers from a normal background will find it difficult to imagine that none of the brethren could even dream about going on a package holiday to the popular resorts in Spain or elsewhere. Even local beaches were to be avoided, as you would be defiled by having to look at those half-naked men and women. And apart from the location even, it was said that the very idea of having a holiday at all was "foreign to the people of God'. On one occasion Peter was present at a picnic on the farm of one of Rachel's relatives, and a crowd of men and women bathed in the river fully clothed rather than expose their flesh and incite lust.

Even in such an environment it is always possible to have special moments. A particular incident from that time stayed in his memory for the rest of his life; one evening, after the meeting and the usual social chat were over, he and Rachel left the children with their grandparents and drove the short distance to the seafront at Lee-on-Solent. Now four years into their marriage, they walked hand in hand along the promenade for quite a while in the warm night air, and as darkness fell they went to the rail and stood together, arms entwined. They gazed out over the calm waters of the Solent; there was a full moon; the town lights shimmered on the Isle of Wight opposite. There were yachts heading for harbour. They just stood there, arms lightly around each other, and for a long time not a single word was spoken. Peter never forgot that moment: that magical feeling of just being with his soulmate; no words were needed, both at some level aware that they were somehow entwined in their very souls.

An interesting feature of the EB was their detachment from certain realities in life that didn't fit what they considered the norm or the Truth.

The example above of the still-born child illustrates their uneasiness about things they couldn't pronounce on with clarity. Mental illness was another issue that they preferred to cordon off. Indeed, one of their Great Men had pronounced that mental illness would not afflict "the people of God". Such a pronouncement sat uneasily with the inevitable experiences of the group, where all of life's rich tapestry was reflected. There was nothing that afflicted "worldly" people that did not also afflict the brethren, and so when something did arise that really "shouldn't have" it was quietly fenced off. A schizophrenic man in Dublin was one such embarrassment for many years, and he was eventually ejected to live rough on the streets, exposed to violent assaults and disease. He was rescued by the Simon Community. This particular case was put to the EB very forcefully by relatives during a time of supposed review in later years and they received a grudging apology.

Peter remembered being surprised to learn how many brethren were killed in bombing raids during WW2, for instance. The very special saints of God were allowed to die in bombing raids? Other events or conditions that fit the category of what shouldn't happen to the saints included murder, suicide, alcoholism, homosexuality, child abuse, incest, wife-beating, and indissoluble marriages that were broken underneath. None of this is any different from the rest of society and it puzzled Peter for many years, though as usual he put it to the back of his mind. The brethren answer would be that they always "dealt with" wrong stuff when it arose, in contrast to other churches and to society as a whole that just accepted it. However, in many cases this "dealing with" matters simply involved ejecting a wrongdoer or a misfit from the fellowship and abandoning them to their fate. In the case of homosexuality, it involved wrong thinking altogether, as it was viewed as a sinful choice. At any rate, in practical terms, the EB society was never at any one time without the same flaws as the rest of the world they were separating from.

CHAPTER 5
Alan and Liz

Alan was Peter's elder brother. They were of a similar nature, both introspective and serious about life. Alan's wife Liz had been cut off from her father and her sisters within weeks of her marriage, because of the new schism that had resulted from the MOG's shenanigans in 1970. Her father and sisters had joined those who did not accept the MOG's behaviour and left the fellowship. She had the choice of staying with Alan, or ending her marriage to return to her family. It would be many years later before Peter would reflect on the anguish that she and others went through at this time. Human feelings were not encouraged, and at this time Peter was as unfeeling and hypocritical as they come. The Truth was above all natural emotion, especially if wasn't affecting you personally.

Alan never seemed to have any doubts about the brethren culture. He read all the books, drank in all the doctrines without question, and was rather obviously ambitious about becoming a leader. Something in his nature simply resonated with the "Truth" that only the brethren knew. Much of this truth was at first similar to all fundamentalist christianity. Man had a sinful nature from birth which was in constant conflict with God; only by repenting and trusting in the shed blood of Christ for redemption could anyone avoid being lost for eternity in the torture of Hell. Jesus is the mediator between God and Man. He accepted the wrath of God on our behalf and in dying on the cross became the Saviour of the human race.

But many older brethren members were secretly uneasy at the new truths that were being pushed on them at this time. No longer was it enough to believe in Jesus to be saved; there was now another mediator as well, the Man of God. Simple worldly christians might cling to their faith in Jesus, but for advanced saints like the EB there was much more. God had provided a man to represent him on earth. This man was now said to be the Personification of the Holy Spirit, as well as successor to the Apostle Paul, through the line picked up by Darby, and the EB leaders who followed, and he was now often referred to simply as 'our Paul'. Alan was one of many young men who now pushed this doctrine relentlessly and he did it with complete conviction. Peter pushed it too, but with the usual deep doubts strongly repressed. Rachel didn't doubt it, but in her usual way she was neutral and didn't really think very deeply about it at all. Liz had her doubts but her very marriage depended on her keeping quiet about them. These four close family members were a microcosm of EB life, pursuing similar lives on the surface but with hidden fault lines underneath that would in time shake them to their foundations. For the moment they remained unaware of the storms to come that would tear some of them apart.

It was this doctrine that led to the Man of God becoming all-powerful in the individual lives of members. Almost every detail of daily life was affected. Men had to abandon wristwatches, at least in the meeting; the meeting room clocks were abolished; the mirrors in the cloakroom were removed; men would no longer wear neckties except for business; women would have to wear scarves instead of hats and also wear their hair loose; women were forbidden to live alone; apartments were forbidden. You could still go to the toilet without instructions, but amazingly even the subject of shared sewer pipes was eventually pronounced upon as an issue of separation. Alan was in sales and when calling on clients he was often offered coffee or lunch. Whereas some brethren in that situation would make some excuse or tell a white lie, Alan was honest and had no hesitation in refusing and explaining why he couldn't socialise with worldly people. To soften the implication that he was calling his clients evil, he would explain that because he had to be separate from the world he must of necessity not be defiled by socialising with anyone who was still connected to the world. Clients were usually remarkably tolerant, mocking him behind his back, but as long as he got the order that was all that mattered. To be fair, he did suffer several very disappointing job losses because of his beliefs, and his honesty about his beliefs, and he was often frustrated in trying to establish a decent career.

After a busy day he would return home to Liz who would have his meal ready. As was now the brethren custom, a whiskey or two were usually imbibed to relax, and soon it would be time for the meeting. Monday night was the Prayer Meeting, held at a small subdivision hall for about thirty members. Every brother sat in a front circle and would have to stand one by one and pray aloud, while the sisters sat in a circle behind. In the past prayers would be for the sick, the government and the armed forces, and various topical events, but now it was obligatory to pray specifically for the Man of God. Not to do so would raise eyebrows and you would become an object of 'concern'. Concern was a big word amongst brethren; they were always concerned about someone or something, and if you wanted a peaceful life you tried to avoid that kind of attention. Thus every prayer became almost identical and monotonous. Occasionally one of those little farces would occur that would lighten the mood. A prominent leading brother in

Australia was called Ron Fawkes, and one night a rather simple soul prayed earnestly for "Guy Fawkes" to be prospered in his endeavours. [Guy Fawkes was the notorious figure who tried to blow up the English Parliament in 1605]. There were at that time five brethren sisters in Tehran, Iran, and one brother had recently gone to live there to help the meeting to carry on. It became customary to pray with a straight face for "the brother carrying on with five sisters in Tehran". Tuesday night would be the Ministry Meeting in the main hall: there was no one in charge of this; three men would speak as they were inspired for about fifteen minutes each. Wednesday would be the City Reading, a bible reading chaired by the local leader or someone he might delegate in his place. This was a kind of discussion on a passage of scripture, but nowadays it also had become another forum for idolising the Man of God. There would be similar meetings on all the other days of the week, but Sunday was special.

Sunday began at 6am with the Lord's Supper, or Breaking of Bread, the equivalent of Mass or Holy Communion in other churches of Christendom. It would be in the small subdivisions like the Prayer meeting. It was the most special of all meetings and if you tried to miss it they would come and ring your doorbell to rouse you. This service follows a very precise form and it is something the EB are particularly proud of, believing that the Lord himself is attracted to appear at it in a very special way each week. Even now there will be ex-members who cling to the greatness of the Lord's Supper as a sign of the advanced light given to the brethren movement. The brothers would be in a circle in front surrounded by the circle of sisters behind, a simple table would be in the centre, with the loaf of bread and the silver cup of wine at one end, and the collection basket at the other. A hymn would be sung, and then after an indeterminate pause a brother would be inspired to stand at the table and 'give thanks for the loaf', adding some ideas of his own. Sometimes two brothers would get inspired at the same time, which was embarrassing as they often had their eyes closed and didn't realise until they both began to speak at once. After giving thanks the brother would break the loaf in half and pass it to the sister directly behind his chair. It would then be passed around the sisters' circle, including the small children, each picking a piece off, and then around the brothers and set back on the table. The same brother would then give thanks for the cup and the process would be repeated. Then he would lift the collection basket without comment and it would go around in the same way. Peter remembered being at a breaking of bread as a child when a woman in her dotage dropped her coin into the cup of wine with a loud clang, saying, "There, that gets that over with!" They hesitated for a while but left the coin where it was rather than fish it out, as others had still to have their sip. Another amusing tale was of a meeting in Scotland where it was discovered too late that the loaf was sliced; when they attempted to proceed anyway, an old timer intoned somberly in a thick Scottish accent, "Can it be right to give thanks for a sliced loaf?" In such a staid, religious, repressed atmosphere such little incidents tend to set people off into helpless giggles, and God is not pleased one bit. Or maybe He has a good laugh too? Perish the irreverent thought. Looking back, though, Peter would realise that maybe God *was in the giggles*. The service would then proceed with hymns and thanksgivings interspersed. Every brother was obliged to contribute a thanksgiving and every sister was to suggest a hymn. The precise course of the service never varied, addressing the Lord Jesus at first, then one hymn to the Holy Spirit, then addressing the Father, and finishing with addressing God. It became a ritual that could be rushed through in a little over half an hour, and many were back in bed before 7am. Unfortunately, when you take your children out at that hour for a 6am meeting they simply don't want to go back to sleep when you bring them home.

Their bed rest would be brief anyway as there was a full day's meetings still to go to, with meal breaks in the homes in between meetings which would fill the whole day. The snacks and meals would be accompanied by copious amounts of alcohol, and there would be music from young people playing pianos and guitars, and maybe a drummer or two. Music, even worldly music such as the Beatles, was fine if it was played live, but it was forbidden to have records or prerecorded taped music. Peter always found it very difficult to explain the subtle distinction, not being a Man of God. It applied even to classical music.

CHAPTER 6
Doubts

Several years into his marriage, Peter was becoming increasingly aware of his doubts about the EB. Once married to Rachel he had found a new freedom in himself. Instead of repressing the doubts as he had always done he was now allowing them to surface and linger. The current Man of God seemed angrier than God himself. He was still ruthless in getting rid of people he just didn't like. He would contradict himself even more often than before, even in print, and woe betide anyone who would draw attention to this. "Power corrupts, and absolute power corrupts absolutely." This man was the living proof of that. The Pope in Rome has nominal absolute authority over millions of Catholics, but in practice he is simply ignored by most of them. This MOG had absolute power over maybe less than 40,000 people worldwide but in practice he had more power than the Pope. Peter would wonder if Christianity was really supposed to be this difficult; there was constant soul-searching --self-judgment it was called. Judgment, whether of self or of others was paramount. The scripture said "Judge not, that ye be not judged", but that was one of many verses that the EB simply ignored. They were proud of 'having a judgment' about everybody and everything. The leaders could sum up anyone in seconds, or so they mistakenly believed.

Brethren now regularly took people to court to split up families if one spouse had left, or to seek compensation for being spoken against by one of their enemies. The apostle Paul, in 1 Corinthians 6 v1, says, "Dare any one of you, having a matter against another, go to law before the unjust, and not before the saints?" but once again, although the brethren used to believe this prevented them using worldly courts, it was now ignored. Also, Jesus said in Matthew 5 v11 & 12, "Blessed are ye when men shall revile you, and persecute you, and shall say all manner of evil against you falsely, for my sake. Rejoice and be exceeding glad; for great is your reward in heaven...", but now it seemed the EB were changing the ending to..." for then you can sue them for millions of dollars." Peter read with some surprise the MOG's assertion that it was acceptable to lie so long it was to protect the EB position. It was illustrated and backed up by the scripture where Ahithophel lied to protect King David against the plotting of Absalom [2 Samuel 15]. When some out-of-fellowship members stirred up the Charity Commission to remove financial privileges from the EB because their meetings were not truly public worship, the leaders embarked on a propaganda crusade that lied openly and said the EB weren't really *that* separate, a totally opposite message to what was going on inside.

Peter slowly realised that he had always been bending his mind to believe opposing viewpoints and realities. It was a feature of life in a system that was full of inconsistencies. He was reminded of Orwell's Animal Farm, as new rules were rolled out that contradicted everything that had been believed before; and sometimes of Alice in Wonderland when you had to believe several different things before breakfast, and words took on whatever meaning the Man of God gave them. On one occasion he was present at a large meeting where the MOG harangued the congregation in a bad-tempered speech to rival a Hitler rant in its sound and fury. It was a seminal moment in his life; as he listened to the rant a great sense of calm seemed to enter his soul. He was emboldened in that moment to think the unthinkable: spiritual power doesn't manifest itself in fury and sound; this man is not what he says he is; this EB movement is not what I thought it was; this surely is not Christianity as it was intended.

Anyone who has exited from a cult, for this in Peter's opinion was now his position, will know the fear and the confusion when you first start to see through what you had always accepted as Truth. The EB were the supposed guardians of High Truth, yet now they seemed barely acquainted with ordinary truth if it didn't suit their purpose. Peter began to challenge some of the members to explain the anomalies, but always the answer was "The Man of God must know best. We just have to bow to his judgment". He would now openly share his doubts at home with Rachel who would be troubled by his thoughts. "You think too much" was her usual response. To speak against the Man of God was likened to the one unforgivable 'sin against the Holy Spirit', a very serious act that would result in you going to Hell [see Matthew 12 v32]. Yet the doctrine had always been that once you were saved you couldn't be unsaved. Ah...but if you speak against the MOG then you were probably never saved in the first place. There was always an answer, and if you could keep bending your mind then you were fine.

Peter no longer wanted to bend his mind around contradictory rules and regulations. He felt his mind must be already twisted into knots after years of doing it. At home and with a few members, emboldened by his clearer thinking, he would now openly speak against the MOG. Rachel would be truly afraid, and the other members would shrink away from him. No one wanted to be around when the lightning bolt destroyed him from the heavens. Yet no lightning bolt came. The knots in his mind began to loosen and unravel bit by bit. He began to read novels, ordinary thrillers, history books, religious books, philosophy books, and current affairs magazines. He bought a small transistor radio and listened to the news and to comedy shows. Many readers will simply not comprehend the significance of such a trivial act; yet it was a major breakthrough, like smuggling a woman into a monastery. Sometimes instead of attending the meeting he would go to the cinema or the pub, with Rachel at home with the children and unaware of his true destination. He was uneasy about deceiving her even in this small way, but he told himself that she simply would not be able to handle it.

Rachel herself knew that Peter was no longer committed to the brethren life, and she was fearful of the consequences. If he was withdrawn from then she would have to make a choice to either stay with her husband, and be cut off from her friends and relatives, or separate from him and stay with her friends in the EB. There was no in-between. She knew at times that he had not been at the meeting he was supposed to be at, and he would smell of drink and smoke sometimes that meant he had been at a pub instead. He thought she didn't suspect anything because she never asked, but the truth was she didn't ask because she didn't want to hear the answer. He would talk more and more about current affairs and ideas that she had no knowledge of and no interest in. She knew she should report his activities to the 'priests', the unofficial guardians of the assembly, but to do so would only hasten the end. So she stayed with her fears and prayed that Peter would see the Light and return to the life he had been called to.

Seven years passed like this. Gradually Peter had carefully unravelled the knots in his mind, strand by strand, and by now he was almost completely free from all brethren brainwashing. He often found more wisdom and inspiration from watching a good film at the cinema than in listening to the daily stream of ministry, yet the EB were convinced that all cinema and theatre were evil. Darby himself had even lambasted Shakespeare's work as uninspired "buffoonery". The next step was to find the courage to leave the fellowship, but the thought of what leaving the fellowship would do to Rachel troubled him intensely. Periodically he would receive 'priestly visits' from concerned elders who would try to convince him to recommit himself to the brethren way of life. In the earlier times he was polite and lied and promised to do better, but now he openly expressed his opinions to them and virtually dared them to withdraw from him. They too were in a dilemma, wanting very much to purge the assembly of this defiant sinner, but unwilling to plunge Rachel into the trauma of having to split up the family.

Every few years in the brethren there would be a witch-hunt instigated to ferret out any corruption that might have crept in. This was dealt with in mass public confessions of various wrongdoings. You didn't have a confession booth like the Catholics; you confessed through the microphone to the full congregation. About this time such a witch-hunt became so frenzied that some people confessed to things they hadn't done just so they didn't feel left out. Elders would visit the homes and hear the stories in great detail. It was obvious that many of these elders enjoyed themselves going over sexual details in particular. Men and women of all ages confessed publicly to masturbation, a sin so shockingly widespread that it was named as a plague; a dignified old lady surprised everybody with a confession of a secret lesbian affair in her youth; a surprising majority of couples confessed to premarital sex; some confessed to 'unnatural sex', mercifully not specified; parents who had ruled their children with a rod of iron were embarrassed to reveal their own youthful indiscretions. It was a form of mass hysteria. The practice of using the shut-up procedure to check for facts now evolved into a method of punishment, with people being shut up for seven days even though they had voluntarily revealed all. Around this time the wedding of Prince Charles and Diana took place, and hundreds of brethren were shut up for watching the ceremony on TVs in shop windows. Neither Peter nor Rachel got involved in this frenzy, although they had been involved in a lesser one shortly after they were married. Because of Peter's current obvious lack of commitment it was viewed with great suspicion that he had apparently nothing to confess, but he was long past caring. To him it simply proved that brethren members were human after all, just like everybody else, and they had no grounds for separating themselves from the rest of humanity. For her part, although Rachel usually acquiesced in whatever the brethren set on, she never felt the need to rake over her past and expose it to public scrutiny. She never confessed to past "sins" unless someone else mentioned her as a participant in theirs, and even then she only acknowledged as little as possible. It was one rule she never took to, despite all her other devotions, and the brethren forever remained unaware of her "colourful" past. It was only colourful, of course, in the sense that it did not conform to their world of black and white. Even pink is colourful in that sort of context, and there is no intention here of painting her as a scarlet woman. She wasn't.

One man was shut up for weeks for having an aerial on his car--he had removed the radio but not the aerial, and this was not enough--the aerial was the "appearance of evil". Another man died in Belfast during his long period of being shut up, and the MOG pronounced that it was a very serious thing to die while shut up. When a local brother repeated this judgment, Peter asked him to explain what was meant--would the man [a] be delayed getting his place in heaven, [b] go straight to hell [c] go to a place specially reserved for people who were shut up when they died? The only reply was that the MOG must know what he was talking about. The fact that he might not know what he was talking about was never considered. Ironically the sin for which this particular man had been shut up was for saying derogatory things about the aforementioned Henry, who had not yet been exposed as an adulterer.

Those who were considered ready were brought before the assembly to confess to their sin and were forgiven. However, unlike most churches even of a fundamentalist nature, the EB held that certain sins left you with a "defect". Adultery and business failure were two of these sins. Having a defect meant that certain limitations were put upon you as to testifying in public for instance, or to conducting a meeting. It was based on Leviticus; an old testament law being carried forward into modern usage. Most Christians would disagree with putting conditions on forgiveness like this.

CHAPTER 7
Exit

Every day Peter dreamed of being free, but it would be such a major step. One Sunday with a houseful of brethren visitors his six-year-old son ran into the room with the transistor radio blaring. Peter froze; the visitors looked shocked; recovering his aplomb Peter seized the radio and pretended that his little boy must have got it from someone at school. Tut tut, you couldn't watch children these days. Whether they believed this or not he never knew, but nobody reported it. He was walking a tightrope, wanting to fall off, but afraid of the consequences. About to exit from the cinema one evening he spied several EB cars stopped at the traffic lights just outside. He spun around quickly and dived inside, much to the puzzlement of the other cinema-goers. Readers who have had reasonably normal lives will wonder how this could be, but this was what was known as a double life!

The situation resolved itself one day in a farcical manner that would further illustrate the bizarre nature of the EB reality. One Wednesday evening Peter drove to the main central meeting hall to attend the City Reading as he was obliged to do. On the journey across the city he saw and was seen by many other members going the same way. Rachel was at home with the children, now four in number. As he would often do nowadays he had fortified himself with whiskey to prepare himself for the grinding boredom of the meeting at which the same old banal mantras about the MOG would be trotted out. He found it helped to be in a bit of a daze, even though he was taking a huge risk in drink-driving. Nevertheless, when he arrived at the meeting hall that night, something inside him just rebelled and he thought "I just can't take any more of this"; he drove on past. Nearby, about a mile or more along the main road, he came to a large exhibition hall and noticed it was staging an Ideal Home Exhibition. Feeling frustrated and with no idea what to do for the rest of the evening, he parked up and went to the exhibition. Later, driving home from there, he was again seen by other members returning from the meeting. Some eagle-eyed members noticed that they had seen him going to and apparently coming from, but not actually attending, the meeting. In your world dear reader this is small stuff. In this EB world it is very serious. A matter of grave concern.

The following Friday in the subdivisional meeting the main theme was about people not attending the meetings. It is a well-worn custom among many forms of brethren to not speak directly to erring members at first, but to subtly or not so subtly 'get at them' in a meeting. Peter was present and aware of who the remarks were aimed at, but had no intention of rising to the bait. However, his father, bless him, on this occasion felt the need to defend his son and caused quite a commotion by challenging what was being said. His mother then got angry about it all and stormed out of the meeting in a very marked manner before it had ended. Peter meanwhile sat through this unperturbed. This kind of scenario was relatively common in brethren meetings from time to time as the lid would blow off hidden frustrations.

The result of this event was that Peter's father was withdrawn from the next morning for 'being contentious', a very useful catch-all phrase for when you wanted to boot somebody out. Peter's mother was 'shut up' --the halfway house between being in fellowship and out of fellowship. In this position you were still a member but you could not attend meetings or communicate with other members, except to the priests or elders who came to visit you to check if you were ready to resume your privileges. Many people languished in the shut-up limbo for months or even years at times.

The rest was a kind of domino effect. Peter was in business with his brother and his father. On Monday morning the immediate challenge from Alan was for Peter to clarify his position. A director could not remain part of the company if he was out of fellowship. Their father would therefore have to resign from the business. Peter had thought about this scenario over the weekend and he now declared that he would stand by his father and that Alan could do as he wished. Neither Peter nor his father were asking Alan to resign from the business. Alan raged at him, shouting that he was going to hell.

The next night therefore, as a result of this decision, Peter was withdrawn from, with Rachel and the children being 'shut up'. In the space of seven days a simple unplanned non-attendance at the meeting had resulted in this drastic action that split a family apart. True, Peter's increasing lack of commitment over the years had contributed to it, but it was still an example of the harsh enforcement of petty rules that had blighted many lives in the past. Was this really Christianity? On one level Peter was relieved to be free at last; on another level he feared what he was letting himself in for. Rachel was devastated. This was the moment she had refused to allow in her imagination for years, even though it was pretty inevitable. Alan felt the glow of his own courageous righteousness in separating from his father and his brother 'for the sake of the Truth', yet also felt deeply saddened and emotional that it had come to this. Liz was a close friend to her sister-in-law Rachel and was appalled, though having no doubt that the real villain was Peter in the whole sorry business. There was no grey area in brethren opinion; there was only right and wrong, black and white, and they were proud of it. The brethren were right and every one who differed was wrong. It was even said by the MOG at one stage that as a member of the brethren 'even when you're wrong you're right', meaning that even an EB member in the wrong was superior to any non-member in the right.

CHAPTER 8
Two worlds collide

This was to be one of the most testing periods of Peter and Rachel's lives, and the full effect of it never really went away. They loved each other deeply, yet their paths were set in distinctly different directions that if followed would lead them to destroy their relationship. What happens when an irresistible force meets an immovable object? Peter knew with complete certainty that he could not return to the EB, and he knew why, and could explain it clearly. Rachel knew with the same certainty that it was wrong to leave the true fellowship, though unfortunately she could not explain why, beyond a shrug and 'just because'. Contrary to EB belief about Peter it was not stubbornness or pride. It was not seeking after a worldly life or an easy life, of which they were accusing him. It was simply that he had outgrown the whole culture. He had changed inside, changed his entire belief system. So far, he still believed there might be a genuine version of Christianity, and he now set himself to research the history of the Church for himself.

Meanwhile he purchased a TV set for the first time in his life. Even in his newly liberated state this felt very strange, such was the extreme horror with which brethren held both TV and radio. It was apparently a pipeline of filth into the home, though Peter couldn't actually find any filth so far. There was a gentle comedy series on at that time with the theme tune, "Love is like a butterfly", and to this day, almost 30 years later, that tune revives for Peter the very strange emotions of that time. To Rachel it was a horrible alien thing, standing there in the corner defiling the home. It made her feel sick at heart, afraid of God's anger and retribution, and afraid of the future. To make matters worse Peter was often angry with her now and she longed for the gentle and kind friend he had once been. He would argue about theological doctrines, trying to explain his thinking logically, but she had never known about doctrines and could only stare wordlessly at him with incomprehension. This frustrated him even more and he would sometimes storm off out, maybe not returning until very late, and sleeping on the couch.

The elders kept up the pressure on Rachel, visiting her during the daytime when Peter was at work. They urged her to stand firm and to separate from Peter and take the four children with her. She was offered financial support.

It was her duty to be faithful to God and to his people above all else. The Truth was greater than any marriage or natural happiness. This was a harsh unbending principle, that the Truth took precedence over natural human or family feelings. She would be rewarded in her soul if she left the marriage and stayed in the true fellowship. She listened to them and she believed they were telling the truth. Yet when they had gone and she thought about leaving Peter she sobbed uncontrollably. She wished with all her heart that he would see the light and get back to his roots in the EB, but even so she could not contemplate leaving him. She knew women in her situation who had left their husbands for this same reason and many of them were bitter and alone with no prospect of another relationship. You couldn't divorce and remarry in the EB. It would be a kind of perpetual enforced widowhood, worse than a real widowhood that at least left you free to remarry. But this was not even relevant to her at this time. Peter was the love of her life, even if he was becoming a stranger to her at the moment, and she couldn't imagine ever wanting anyone else.

At night she would lie beside him sobbing audibly but he did not respond. It was very hard for him to do this but the only thing she wanted from him that would stop her tears was the one thing he couldn't give. In the morning he would tell her to do what she thought was right; go back to the brethren and I will get out of your life. He was as terrified of losing her as she was of losing him, but he could not return to the brethren without losing his very soul, or descending into insanity.

In a few months she made her courageous decision and the brethren sorrowfully withdrew from her, though still regarding her as the victim of an evil man. Peter was enormously relieved and though still frustrated by her air of martyrdom he began to soften his attitude to her. He made an effort to try to understand the trauma from her point of view. After all, just because he had changed his beliefs didn't mean Rachel had to change her beliefs as well. She was her own person and she was an equal, not a subservient wife as he had once thought of her. It would be many years before he truly understood this and it was a major step in his soul's progress. When he looked back a few years later, he could see that his angry outbursts and often impatient aggressiveness at this period had been a very strange way indeed to try and convince her that he was on the right path.

CHAPTER 9
Christianity

"We believe in God, the Father, the Almighty, maker of heaven and earth, of all that is seen and unseen. We believe in one Lord, Jesus Christ, the only Son of God, eternally begotten of the Father, God from God, Light from Light, true God from true God, begotten, not made, one in being with the Father. Through Him all things were made. For us men and our salvation He came down from heaven: by the power of the Holy Spirit, He was born of the Virgin Mary, and became man. For our sake He was crucified under Pontius Pilate; He suffered, died, and was buried. On the third day He rose again in fulfilment of the scriptures: He ascended into heaven and is seated at the right hand of the Father. He will come again in glory to judge the living and the dead, and his kingdom will have no end. We believe in the Holy Spirit, the Lord, the giver of life, who proceeds from the Father and the Son. With the Father and the Son, he is worshipped and glorified. He has spoken through the Prophets. We believe in one, holy, catholic, and apostolic Church. We acknowledge one baptism for the forgiveness of sins. We look for the resurrection of the dead, and the life of the world to come. Amen."

This is a copy of the Nicene Creed, drafted in 325AD and finally settled in 381AD. The first draft stopped at "We believe in the Holy Spirit", and much argument took place before deciding that the Holy Spirit should be worshipped and glorified in the same way as Father and Son.

Peter was of an inquisitive nature, and he had always enjoyed reading history. He now delved into the history of Christianity with the intention of identifying a church that still practised it as it had been established by Jesus and the apostles. There had always been mention in the EB of the pristine church that had existed before the breakdown. However, the more he read the more astonished he became. It surprised him that many of the central doctrines of Christianity had only been settled on after long debates over centuries and often by majority vote. On at least one occasion the vote was carried by the Roman emperor who wasn't even Christian. The bible itself had been assembled in this way, with many available books rejected and others selected after long arguments. The bible was supposed to be the abiding Word of God, complete for all time, not to be tampered with. You could

44

trust the Word of God. But now logically, it seemed to Peter, since the bible was in fact a man-made selection of books, a selection arrived at by majority vote, you were putting your trust in the bishops who assembled it rather than in God. Reading the history of that time does not inspire much confidence in the integrity of the bishops. To Peter, this was a stunning revelation. The four gospels were accepted into the canon in the second century AD, several decades after the crucifixion. Mark, regarded as the earliest to be written was written about 70 AD, almost forty years after the events depicted. It was only in the fourth century AD that Revelation was finally accepted into the canon. As to the gospels, how accurate were the stories of what Jesus actually said? They were not exactly verbatim records. Perhaps the most unsettling insight of all that came to him was that the bible as a unit is in many ways a deception: it is a collection of books deliberately selected and assembled to give the impression that it represents the sum of God's communications to Man over the ages. Somehow we all conspire to ignore the yawning gap between the angry, violent Jehovah of the Old Testament, and the loving and forgiving Jesus in the New. How do those two co-exist in the same book, even separated into "Testaments"? Peter recognised once again the old practice of bending ones mind around awkward inconsistencies.

Many Christians in more liberal churches may not see anything strange in some of these facts. Peter however had always thought that the principles of Christianity had been directly inspired by God, and were absolute truth. He had assumed, certainly very naively, that the bible was a seamless history of the world since time began. But this belief was not uncommon amongst many Christians, and was certainly regarded as orthodoxy in many versions of the PB. Darby's writings had outlined a structure of seven 'dispensations', roughly one-thousand year periods of history, from the creation in 4004 BC onwards that would be completed with the thousand years rule of Christ on earth, known as the Millennium.

Peter could now see that the strict ideas of separation that the EB practised had come down directly from the Jewish laws; Christianity had not been a truly fresh start from Heaven, as he had believed, but a gradual evolving offshoot of the Jewish faith. Many ideas from Greek philosophy and other ancient religions had been woven in to create a new faith far removed from any words that Jesus had actually spoken. Ancient feast days, both religious and profane, had been adapted to take on new Christian significance, to become what we now celebrate as Easter, Epiphany and Christmas and many others. Artists had created their own ideas of Mary and her Child, the last Supper, and many other of the biblical stories, giving a new form to old traditions that became accepted as fact. The wise men, not numbered in the bible, became three, and even got names: Caspar, Melchior and Balthasar.

Strange as it may seem, Peter was seeing for the first time how these ideas had gradually evolved into what became the new Christian religion. Control of the masses became a goal for the bishops and priests; the Roman Empire in its weakening state had embraced the religion for its own militaristic purposes, and as a result the bishops became wealthy and powerful. One of the best ways to keep people in line was to instil fear in them: if you stray from the Christian faith you will burn in everlasting Hell. It seemed that perhaps the majority of Christians just accepted the stories without ever questioning their origin, or looking at how the stories had changed over the centuries. At the Reformation the Protestant movement did overthrow a lot of the practices which had enriched the priests, including the sale of indulgences for the forgiveness of sins. Yet it had still retained the basic structure of Christianity. Now all this is fine for anyone who feels they want to be part of a dynamic living religion that changes with the times. But it was very disturbing to a man like Peter who had been taught that the Truth was absolute, unchanging, completely revealed for all time. Now it seemed to him that Christianity was just another religion in the same mould as Islam, Hinduism, Buddhism, or indeed any of the thousands of belief systems down the ages. The pristine church that the EB claimed to have rediscovered had never existed in the first place. The sense of the Divine authority of the Christian faith over his soul was now lost. Once again in his life he was having to think the unthinkable.

As we have seen, the history of the EB was strewn with schisms about doctrinal matters. The "Eternal Sonship question" was one of the early ones and meetings split away on one side or the other. Peter now found that the same argument had been going on since the early days of Christianity. Was Jesus the Son of God for all of a past eternity, or just from the time of his birth on earth? There was no answer to this, yet fierce intellectual battles were fought over it. Each side always claimed to have the Truth. The question about whether the Holy Spirit should be worshipped or not was another reason for EB schism, yet this was obviously a centuries-old argument as well, as we can see from the Nicene Creed.

CHAPTER 10
Making a new life

Rachel continued to believe that the brethren were God's special people. She could not explain why this was so. As with many things in her life she just accepted what was, because that was always how it had been. Though she had lost her place in the fellowship through her loyalty to her husband, she carried on with an inner conviction that if she remained faithful to the Truth God would rescue her by somehow changing Peter's mind. The elders had urged this path on her in their final appeals to her. So she dreamed of the day they would be received back into fellowship. She never watched TV or took any more interest in world affairs than she ever had. She was busy as a full-time mother of four children. She secretly tried to keep the children separate from some events at school, but it was a losing battle. The children soon knew that an appeal to their father would allow them their freedom. Relations with Peter were less strained and they were still very much in love underneath the disagreement about religion. Another child was born less than two years after they had left the fellowship.

Because Peter's business had been divided up unnaturally in order to suit the separation rules for his brother, it slowly ran out of steam and went bankrupt. This was regarded by some as the "government of God". It may not have been clearly spelled out as this, and would not have been motivated by spite or malice in any case. The brethren were singleminded and they thought it perfectly acceptable to see someone driven into the ground if it would help to bring them crawling back to the fellowship and to save their souls. Peter himself was once that type of person who thought like that. Rachel was not that cruel but she still hoped for the same result. So she gave very little moral support to Peter as he went through the humiliation of meeting angry creditors and bankers and bailiffs. They had their two cars repossessed from the driveway, and only just managed to hold on to the house because there was no equity worth seizing.

However, when she saw the characteristic determination in his demeanour she soon realised that even this catastrophe would not shake him into a return to the fellowship. For the first time she began to wonder if maybe his path was indeed a principled one; he really believed in what he was doing and wasn't just a 'backslider' as the elders were alleging. In her heart she softened her attitude towards him, beginning to accept the very remote possibility that he wasn't under the power of the devil after all. As she softened in this subtle way she found he became less belligerent and she caught glimpses of the old gentle nature that she loved. The expected downward spiral of Peter into debauchery and sin that the elders had predicted just wasn't happening. As he became freer and freer of religious pressure he seemed much happier and contented. He was devoted to the children and was never happier than when simply spending evenings at home with them.

Life continued therefore on a fairly peaceful path, but there were underlying currents that would yet cause trouble. Rachel had refused to attend any other church from the outset, except once or twice under protest. The EB had the most peculiar and extreme condemnation of other churches, to the extent that they would rather see you go to a cinema, which was definitely evil, than to see you join another fellowship. Joining another church was somehow the final rejection of the special Light that had been vouchsafed to the People of God. Peter soon stopped asking her to go to church and she was relieved. Now she wondered if it had been wise of her to reject another church. For now it was worse: he was openly rejecting Christianity itself, and that was scary. She mused on the irony of two people being so much in love who were so different in so many ways. Rachel didn't like to think about things at all much, beyond what was visible and accepted; Peter could never stop thinking about everything and anything, both visible and invisible.

It was when he would try to introduce her to new friends that friction once again resulted. It was one thing to have this peaceful home life built on an unspoken compromise, but for Rachel the idea of making new friendships outside of the fellowship was a step too far. Subconsciously she knew such a move would make their position more permanent, and she had not stopped dreaming of a return to the old life. Every time she would go out with Peter to meet other couples she would quietly sabotage the evening by being politely withdrawn and unfriendly. It worked, and gradually Peter gave up. It is easy to judge her harshly for her behaviour, but look at how many people in all walks of life cling to outdated beliefs and myths. Fear of the unknown makes people cling to their comfort zone. Many people in the brethren movement and elsewhere prefer to have someone else define what is right and wrong for them, thus avoiding the need to think for themselves.

CHAPTER 11
More fault lines

One Christmas one of the children received a radio as a present from a distant relative, and once again Rachel bristled and created an atmosphere. Peter began to despair. It was now nine years since they had left the EB and although Rachel was more relaxed it seemed she was no nearer to letting them go after all. She was still the righteous wife, keeping the faith secretly until the Lord would work his miracle and restore them happily to the fellowship.

It was almost too much for him to contemplate that her mind would never change, but he had to accept reality and over the next few months he resolved to leave her and begin a new life unencumbered by the past. One Sunday he approached her away from the children and told her that he would leave her for good in one week unless they could resolve their differences. Rachel was shocked beyond belief, yet she knew by now that when Peter said something he always carried through, and there was that steely determination now in his manner. She asked him if he still loved her and was chilled to the bone when he said no. He added that he didn't rule out being able to love her again if they could come to a proper resolution about the EB. Deep down he knew he still loved her and always would, but he was frustrated beyond reason. He felt that his wife's heart belonged to another, not like to a man she was having an affair with, but worse than that. Meanwhile it was only fair that if she was determined to stand by her beliefs, and he was determined to stand by his beliefs, then he would stand aside and she could return to the fellowship she was pining for, and take the children also. Somebody had to give in. He had no idea of what he would do beyond leave the house and try to start a new life.

Whether it was her characteristic refusal to think about what was happening or whether she really did consider letting him leave was unclear. By the following Sunday she had given him no indication that she would make any effort to resolve the matter. His heart was heavy. He really hadn't banked on her doing this, although he would keep his word whatever it cost. He could not accept a life that was still so effectively hobbled by the EB even if it was indirectly and from a distance. He had told her that even if he was to become a Christian again tomorrow he would still not ever return to the distorted version of Christianity that was the EB.

It was late Sunday afternoon when he took a wedding photo of theirs and cut it in two, handing her portion to her, and saying goodbye. For such a gentle man at heart Peter could be utterly and coldly ruthless when roused. Rachel flinched visibly and went pale. Yet still she said nothing. He asked for her wedding ring back and she gave it to him. He said he would keep it as a memento of their good times together, and that he was off to pack some clothes and set out to find another life and another partner. He wondered what on earth he was going to say to the children. This couldn't be happening. How could his wife really prefer such a weird cult that she didn't even understand, to a loving marriage that was capable of generating so much joy? And it was a loving marriage. Love is not always a fairy-tale romance; love is deeper than that.

He went out to the garden to think. He was not retreating from his position. He felt he was being fair by all standards in that he was releasing Rachel to pursue her own principles. In a more normal church she could simply have continued her membership and stayed married to him, but the EB would not accept that. And so insidiously the EB was still reaching its evil tentacles into his life through Rachel. Years later he wondered, when he was pondering the nature of unconditional love, whether his actions at this time were justified. She had as much right to stand by her own beliefs as he had. In his heart he knew he had lied about not loving her, that he still loved her as much as ever, and that he always would. Yet at this time he thought her behaviour was unreasonable. Many couples in similar circumstances had broken up. There is no manual on how to behave properly in these matters.

He went inside. It felt like he was once again in a nightmare and he wished he could wake up from it. As he headed for the stairs Rachel was coming down. He noticed she was wearing her very best clothes, and her hair was freshly brushed, framing her face as he loved it, and she was to him just stunningly beautiful. She came down to him and took his hand and led him into the empty sitting room. They looked into each other's eyes and she clung to his hand. She said, "I love you Peter, and I can't give up my marriage for the EB. I have made that decision. I can't bear the thought of you being with someone else. I want us to be truly happy again and I will work it out with you if you will allow me." Peter gazed back at her and he wanted to believe her. "Rachel, it's been nine years now. If you couldn't shake it off in nine years how will you do it now? I can't let you just stall me and string me along. I will not allow the EB to impinge on my life for a second longer. You would have to fully accept that we are never going back there, and stop secretly pining to go back."

As they talked Rachel eventually convinced him that she would change her outlook. Peter agreed that he would make some compromises and that he would stop criticising the EB in her hearing. He would agree that neither of them would mention them, and they would build a new life with none of the old influences or any mention of any kind of imposed rules. They talked for a long time, and they finally knew they had once again overcome another huge obstacle in their life. Peter was vastly relieved. In later life he wondered at his behaviour at this time. Was he just being controlling, demanding obedience? Some readers will think so, but life is not that simple. He had still a lot to learn and unlearn about unconditional love. As he looked back over the years he knew that he would not have been able to stay away from her in any case. But whether he acted rightly or not, the crisis did help in greatly reducing the influence of the EB in their lives.

Rachel was true to her word and she did her best to build a new life that was free of the old fears and restrictions. She even began to watch some TV and got to like her own favourite programmes. Ironically by now Peter was finding that a lot of TV was really boring anyway, but it was good to see her acting more naturally. He responded to her new mood and their love deepened as each year passed. He knew that deep down Rachel still couldn't really make friends with 'worldly' people beyond being polite and helpful when she met them, so he gave up trying to form new friendships and just immersed himself in family life. He enjoyed her companionship immensely and it was enough, along with the delight he took in the children. He had started a new business and soon he was making enough money to take the family on holidays abroad. This was something you could never do as an EB member, where all holidays were taboo, and it was doubly exciting for Peter to at last see the world as never before. On those holidays Rachel would be at her best, with not a trace of the old anxieties. He realised with sudden insight that there had never been any EB instructions on how to behave on a holiday abroad, because it was forbidden in the first place. Thus Rachel was able to subconsciously relax completely, having had no programming for this experience.

After a few years of being out of fellowship Peter's father decided to return to it. His mother was not minded to go with him, because as we have seen their marriage had always been very tempestuous. In order for him to be received back in fellowship the brethren insisted on a legal separation through the courts. They drew up papers for the separation, citing the reason as "withdrawing from iniquity". The brethren's solicitor contacted Peter for some reason, rather than his mother, probably because he was already acquainted with him. Peter objected strongly to allowing the separation to go through on the basis of withdrawing from iniquity; he knew that his parents should have separated many years ago for the simple reason that they did not get on, but it was dishonest to put it through as a religious problem. The brethren would not have allowed divorce or separation in the normal way, that is, as a simple acknowledgment of the breakdown of a relationship. Only when it came to accepting one spouse to remain in fellowship and the other out, would they allow it, and then insist on the legal separation in the guise of it being done "for the Truth". Under Peter's influence and resistance the process became very lengthy, with several court hearings before the somewhat puzzled judges got fed up with it and it was finally granted. His father went to live with Alan, and Peter never saw him again. When he died, Alan informed his mother only, not Peter or his sister; and he only informed his mother **after** the funeral was over. No doubt this was to ensure that the out-of-fellowship members of the family would not sully the funeral with their presence. It transpired that he had been ill for months before his death but whether he ever asked to see his other family is not known.

Many years later the EB under a new MOG set up a "Review" of the past and they sent apologies to many former members for their cruel behaviour. They succeeded in bringing back a few ex-members, but not on the scale they were possibly expecting. Peter and Rachel were approached to see if they might consider going back, but in their case there was no apology for any of the harsh treatment. Peter wasn't looking for an apology anyway. He had known what he was getting into when he took the step to leave. Their reasoning was dishonest; they blamed all the excesses on the ordinary brethren, yet all those actions had been specifically approved by the leader at the time, who was claiming to be speaking on God's behalf. Some of the actions had even been initiated by the leader in very clear terms. Nothing was ever done without consulting the leader. It was another "Animal Farm" type of manoeuvre: the MOG had been misinterpreted and misrepresented, they said, and the brethren needed to humble themselves. At the very least, how could such a powerful man have not noticed what was going on in thousands of cases around the world? Nobody had dared to act without consulting him. To Peter it seemed that the new MOG was simply stamping his own absolute power on the movement by doing and saying whatever he liked, and by appearing to be meek and mild. The evidence as time went on pointed to a continued policy of simply making up the rules as he went along. You can do that when you are completely unopposed. In fact it actually increases your power, because the people under you now never know what to think, and they have to stop even the little bit of thinking that they had. Just because blue was red yesterday doesn't mean it won't be green tomorrow. If the MOG says so, it is! Don't try to think!

During this Review some EB cousins of Rachel expressed a desire to her to come and visit. Over and over they said, "We want to see Peter". The previous years of complete ostracism were to be forgotten, they said. Yet even this was not what it seemed. Peter was sceptical and he sent word to them through Rachel that they were welcome to come for dinner. "You know we can't do that", was the reply. The visit was to be on their terms alone, as always, and they still wouldn't eat with a non-member, even their beloved cousin Rachel. There was no visit, but that was their decision, not Peter's.

CHAPTER 12
The new Path

There were many years of happy family life. There were six children and the house buzzed with energy and laughter. Rachel was a superb mother, as well as wife, and she worked very hard to take care of everyone's needs. Like most mothers she had to work too hard, and she was taken very much for granted and put upon, and yet she went on without complaint, as again, do most mothers. Aside from her inability to completely reject the EB, she was a truly beautiful soul, and Peter loved her and knew he was lucky to be with her. There were people in her life who completely missed her true character, but she seemed to be able to rise above that.

Peter continued his search for the meaning of life. Christianity was now to him no more than a very powerful story, to be enjoyed around Christmas. He loved the cathedrals, the art and the architecture, and the sense of history connected with the Church. You could not study the history of the western world over the last two thousand years without acknowledging the huge part played by the Church. Some of the its behaviour was undoubtedly appalling, but it also did an enormous amount of good in various ways. It was true that the Church had hoarded fabulous wealth whilst the populace often starved; yet the great cathedrals and monasteries were still inspiring buildings after centuries of use. The Church had looked after the sick and provided education and a framework for society that held it together.

The religions of Islam and Judaism were so closely related to Christianity that they were not an attractive alternative. He attended a meeting of Humanists but found their ideas bleak. The concentration on the human as a being without any purpose beyond this earthly existence seemed devoid of imagination. The eastern religions were interesting but didn't seem to resonate in his soul. In truth he was content to live without a religion; he felt better in himself without the burden of struggling against a supposedly sinful nature. Yet he somehow knew that there had to be more to life than random existence followed by oblivion. It didn't make sense that mankind had built such magnificent civilisations and made such great advances in science, art, architecture and psychology, only for each person to have a brief innings and then vanish for ever.

Around this time Rachel reported seeing a distinct vision of one of her uncles, standing there physically in her kitchen, dressed in work clothes she remembered from her childhood. He did not speak, but just stood smiling at her. She was so startled that she cried out his name. Then he faded away. This uncle was still a member of the EB and she had been cut off from him for years. This was not the sort of thing Rachel would easily believe in, but she was quite sure about what she had seen, and she made no attempt to explain it away. As far as she knew her uncle was still alive in England. On Peter's advice she eventually phoned her father to ask about her uncle's health. Her father told her that her uncle had passed away a few weeks previously. Her uncle had never been to Ireland in his life, never mind in that particular kitchen, so it was no flashback of memory.

Life was good now and so he was in no real hurry to find out what came after death. He settled for agnosticism, with a vague hope that he might discover more at some time in the future. When he thought of dead relatives, especially his father, he wondered if they did still exist, and if they did, in what form. He came upon a book by Raymond Moody, Life after Life, which told stories of "Near-death-experiences", recounting the experiences of many people who had been clinically dead and been revived medically. The stories varied in detail but all told of being out of the physical body and looking down on it. People would describe having watched the doctors working on their body from a position near the ceiling. Many went through a tunnel into the Light and saw dead relatives and kind beings who welcomed them. Some were given a choice as to whether they would return to the body; others were told it was not their time and they would have to return. People from all religions and none were welcomed equally into the Light. He found it intriguing. The scientists who wrote it off as hallucination caused by oxygen deprivation were unconvincing. Why would everybody have the same type of hallucination? Where would such ideas have originated? There were atheists among the ones who had these experiences who certainly expected to see absolutely nothing when they died, so why would they have the same experience as a Christian who was expecting something?

There were TV shows with mediums like Colin Fry, or John Edwards, demonstrating convincingly to members of an audience that their loved ones were not only still alive but still aware of what is going on here on earth. Peter was becoming more and more convinced that life existed after the death of the physical body, but it was still just a matter of interest and curiosity. After one Colin Fry show he wondered aloud to Rachel whether his dad would come through in such a show if he attended one. In spite of the breakdown in their relationship, he always continued to hold a deep affection for his father.

Then one night, out of the blue, in June 2005, Rachel became really ill with a very serious pain in her back. She was one of those people who had rarely been ill at any time in her life. This was really unusual for her to be in such pain. She visited the doctor and they did some tests, and sent away for a scan appointment. Meanwhile she was put on strong painkillers. As is often the case the NHS system produced a date for a scan several months ahead. Her pain worsened and it became necessary to go privately for a scan. The news was devastating. She had cancer, and it was very advanced. It was later thought to have started in the bowel, but by this time it was already in her lungs and her liver.

Peter was devastated and practically went to pieces. It was Rachel who stayed strong for him for a few days until he steadied himself. Two weeks after diagnosis she was taken in to hospital and given chemotherapy. With her family around the bed she was cheerful and joked about her probable demise in a few months. No one thought it was funny. Released from hospital she stayed at home for 10 days. No one knew what to think. Peter browsed on the internet to see if any new cures were available. There were many unscrupulous people offering cures for cancer for large sums of money. He didn't have that kind of money, which was just as well as he would probably have spent any amount on any remotely hopeful cure offered. Rachel seemed to get weaker and weaker, but no one knew if this was a temporary thing before rallying again.

At the end of the ten days she was very weak and in a wheelchair. They went back to the hospital for the assessment of how the chemo had worked. She was assessed and then sent to a private side ward. She and Peter waited for hours for the doctor to come, weary and afraid, still daring to hope but bewildered. When the doctor arrived he indicated that the chemo had not had any effect; he pointed out that he had seen some patients recover from this low point, but that if such was not the case she would have about two weeks to live. He said that now would be a good time to sort out any outstanding matters.

They looked at each other when he had gone, and both said they had nothing to sort out. The atmosphere was surreal. The news that Rachel would pass away within two weeks was almost too much to comprehend. The body and the mind numb themselves at a time like this to prevent a total breakdown. Thousands of people have had this experience and no doubt thousands more will have it in the future, but it is only when it happens to you that the full impact hits you.

Rachel's father was still alive and a member of the EB, and so it became known in that august body of saints that Rachel was dying of cancer. They began phoning Peter to remind him of his duty to return to the fellowship now that God had spoken in such a direct manner. The implication was that

Rachel's illness was God's judgment for Peter's rejection of the Truth. The brethren often spoke about the "government of God" as a sinister force that caught up with you because of your wrongdoing. They didn't say that to Peter in so many words but it was the kind of thing they had often spelled out in the past and it was obvious what they meant. They promised that the whole fellowship would be there to support him through his troubles. They pushed for the right to visit Rachel, as they still regarded her as a victim of Peter's evil course. In their eyes she still really belonged to them. Peter found his old fierce anger against them returning and he refused to allow them to visit. His brother and his wife pushed hard for a visit, though Liz was much more humane and sympathetic than her husband. Alan was totally insensitive, hectoring and arrogant. This, fumed Peter at the time, from the man who years earlier had only reported their father's death AFTER his funeral. The two brothers had the angriest exchange of words of their whole life. Peter spoke derisively about their current Man of God, and Alan said it was blasphemy. It was the first time that he had ever been told that blasphemy applied to a mere man. It was indicative of how the Man of God had evidently now almost become God. Here in the midst of great personal and family sorrow the EB would once again demonstrate their ruthless insensitivity in their so-called commitment to the "Truth" as being above all natural and human feeling. It was fine in their eyes to harass a man in deep distress about losing his wife, in order to prove their own great monopoly on Righteousness and Truth. The support of their great fellowship would as always be on their terms alone.

As Rachel began to fade away she slept more and had no appetite for food. One day as Peter held her hand he said to her, "It looks like you are going on ahead". She shook her head weakly, eyes still closed, and said, "Oh no, Peter, let's go together, just you and me." It was the last thing she said to him before she passed away, as she shortly afterwards slipped into a coma. Sceptics, especially EB sceptics, will say she didn't know what she was saying, but to Peter it meant a lot. No one knows the reality of two people in love except themselves. Ten days after the doctor's pronouncement the family were called to Rachel's bedside to be with her as she passed away. She was for all appearances unaware of them because of the morphine, but Peter and the family had some sense that she knew they were there. Propped up on pillows, she breathed laboriously, slower and slower, until what was to be her very last breath. The family ran out quickly in distress. Peter slipped her wedding ring from her finger and kissed her forehead for the last time, whispering a loving goodbye. It had been only forty five days since her cancer had been diagnosed.

Once again the EB sprang into action demanding the right to organise the funeral. Peter resisted them as politely as he could, though feeling angry and defensive. A very sorrowful time was once again being trodden on with hobnail boots. The funeral service was organised and held in the church to which their son was attached, and attracted a much larger crowd than anyone had anticipated.

Rachel's son and five daughters arranged a service which included a slide show of Rachel's life from childhood to recent months. They composed a tribute to her which was respectful, and at times amusing, as they recalled their mother's little quirks and eccentricities. Peter composed his own tribute. Both tributes were read out by the minister as the family were too emotional. The service was totally different from what a brethren funeral would have been. At their services very little would be said about the individual being buried; it was just another occasion for listening to God's word.

Peter's tribute was:

"The words which come to mind when describing Rachel are:
gentle and kind, loyal and loving, devoted to her husband and family.
She had a simple outlook on life, content and easygoing; taking pleasure in
ordinary everyday family life,
never seemingly finding it a drudge.
This quality radiated a calm contentment to the whole family.
She smiled and laughed a lot, she was fun to be with. Sometimes her own
quirky humour would make her dissolve into helpless laughter,
the memory of which will always bring a smile to those who knew her.
She rarely saw any bad in anyone, and certainly never looked for it;
neither did she enjoy gossip and spite and petty one-upmanship
politics and competition were outside the scope of her understanding.
She was very forgiving and tolerant
and many a time she needed to be,
but she kept the welfare of the family and me as her prime goal
and her even temperament smoothed many a bump on the way.
More seriously, at a time of great crisis in our lives,
when events tested our marriage and family to the limit
threatening to destroy our relationship
Rachel sacrificed her preferred course, and by doing so kept us together,
and we continued as a happy complete family until her passing away.
I want to pay heartfelt tribute to her for that outstanding achievement.
When the doctor gave us the bad news he told us it was time to sort out any
problems we had with each other,
We looked at each other and we couldn't think of anything that needed
sorted.
I had just over 32 years with Rachel and I wish I could have the same again.

But though the sorrow of her passing is bitter
It is more than outweighed by the memories I will always treasure
Of a sweet loving and lovely wife
loyal best friend
and of a life of laughter and fun and easygoing friendship
I was privileged to know her
may she rest in peace.

At the cemetery there was also a large crowd, much to the astonishment of an EB contingent which was standing off separately to one side. After the short service one of the EB asked Peter to speak to his brother. Peter agreed and approached Alan and his wife, offering to shake hands. Alan folded his arms in refusal, saying,"We are only hear to honour Rachel, not you", so Peter turned away and joined the group of people who had come to show their loving support and their human kindness. After the group had dispersed a latecomer witnessed the EB group going to the grave and conducting their own service, no doubt in order to make sure Rachel would reach the right part of heaven, marked "Private, Brethren Only".

PART TWO
Peter takes up his own story:

CHAPTER 13
Mediums

For the next few weeks I was miserable and depressed. As well as experiencing the natural grief of losing my wife I had now descended into a maze of doubt and despair. The old feelings of negativity returned and I began to berate myself for all the times when I had been less than a perfect husband, and they were many. I raged at the universe for the brutal way in which it tore loved ones apart. I wondered at the sheer futility of human life that would always end in death. Whiskey became my companion, to blot out the sorrows and frustrations.

Eventually, in the midst of my confusion, my old fierce curiosity began to assert itself, and I left off the medication. Where had Rachel gone? I had to know. I would talk to her all the time. Sometimes with black humour I would say to her, "Don't think you can get away from me just by dying. I'm going to find you." At times in the night I could sense her presence, could feel her embrace, perhaps even the whisper of a whisper. Yet when I mentioned this to others they just looked at me kindly; poor chap, losing his wife and now losing his mind. Christian acquaintances would assure me that she was "with the Lord", and I understood this to mean that she was safe, but she was asleep awaiting the resurrection at the end of time. While such a reality would be of some comfort I did not feel able to accept it fully. Atheists would say that she had ceased to be, and I should just keep her alive in my memory. I found that even less appealing, and I knew on some deep level that that explanation did not make sense. Life lived for a span of 52 years would be quite pointless if that was all there was to it.

On the internet I began browsing for information about the afterlife. I found a book called 'We Don't Die', about a medium in New York called George Anderson, and I bought it and devoured it in one sitting. Here were really convincing stories of communications from another dimension, really detailed interviews with people who had passed over. I was excited and I searched for more books on the same subjects, finding to my surprise that there were hundreds of them. Some were more convincing than others; some were quite hard to believe, and probably some of them were sheer fantasy. Yet, as I worked my way through them all, the overwhelming evidence was in favour of life continuing after physical death.

The idea of there being communication from the so-called dead is variously mocked and demonised. Both the Jewish religion of the Old Testament, and then the Church, successfully demonised it over many centuries, so that most people fear it as a dark and devilish thing not to be trifled with. Comedians and satirists mock it mercilessly. Many charlatans professing to be mediums have cheated the gullible and brought the whole business into disrepute. There are charlatans in all walks of life, including comedians who are not funny, and Christians who are not what they profess to be, and scientists of doubtful ability, and yet we don't dismiss the real thing because of that. Christians postulate that clever demons are impersonating our loved ones in order to deceive us. Why and how would they do that? Does that make any kind of sense? Although the bible has passages condemning communication with the "dead", it also has the story in 1 Samuel 28 which tells of King Saul engaging the female medium of En-dor to contact the dead prophet Samuel. This contact is successful, and although Samuel is not necessarily pleased at being disturbed in this way by Saul he does talk to him and predicts the outcome of the battle. The question has to be asked: why would a holy prophet respond in this way if it was the work of the devil? Those who take their belief from the bible have a hard time reconciling this.

As is often the case about any matter, people believe what they want to believe. The only way for me to move further was to test it for myself. I had spent too many years under indoctrination, accepting other people's beliefs, and by now I would simply not accept either Christians or atheists telling me what to believe. So in that September I booked a telephone session with George Anderson, the first available date being for the following March. I was now personally convinced of this medium's genuineness and so I didn't take advantage of the option that was offered me of giving a false name and address. The details are handled separately by his staff who then pass only the telephone number to Anderson just before he calls it. The call came through from Anderson in New York to me in Ireland, and it lasted for about one hour. The medium checked that I knew who he was, did not ask my name, and instructed me to give absolutely no help and to say only yes or no or don't know. The detail that then came through was to me stunning, and the main part of it is given here, with comments interspersed:

"Well, immediately a male presence comes forward, but two females follow also, and there does seem to be another male in the background, might be someone of a later generation.......one male comes in a father manner....and there is also your father's father...and also his father too...three generations

[NOTE: My father may have been making the initial connection, or Rachel may have asked him to go first knowing as she did, from my earlier remarks, how I had wanted to hear from him. I personally favour the latter]

....and now one of the females quickly moves forward....and she comes very close to YOU personally....she is there with your dad and the other relatives but she is moving close to YOU personally...and she puts a big heart in front of you...she's telling me she is your sweetheart...she keeps coming to you in a very loving manner...actually she did pass over relatively young..she speaks of her own family on the earth...she identifies herself as wife and mother...she wanted to emphasise first she is your sweetheart because she jokes that anybody can be husband and wife but that doesn't mean they necessarily like each other!

....she is saying there was a lack of communication emotionally with her side of the family...they were not in her life emotionally at one time,
[a reference to the separation as a result of leaving the EB]

She tells me she has not been very long there and is still considered a new arrival....yet she knew she was going to pass on...she is not surprised to be there.....again she draws very close to you so I take it you and she are very close.....again she reaches out to you as your sweetheart, as your wife and as a good friend....she just wants to make sure that no matter what you feel or believe, as long as you hold this truth to yourself, that she knows that you love her and she loves you.....because sadly when you lose your sweetheart you also lose a very good friend...you miss her company as much as anything else...
She says her health problems sneaked up on her very suddenly...by the time it was found it had done its damage...but she does tell me she tried her best to get well....now you are relatively young too....she says if anybody had told you you would be a young widower you would not have believed them...because she says you thought you would go first and you wish you had...but she is a very straightforward woman and she says it is not your time to be there yet. She says it is better to have been together for the time you were than not at all...and she adds that she is very much around you and your family ..which I suspect you already realise...
Now her mother is there with her...that's your mother-in-law! Also George is there and says he is with your wife and family...he and your wife are very close over there and he says to tell you that "your loss is my gain!"
[George is my father, and this is exactly the kind of quip he would make]

Your wife was saying that she is walking fine again and she is back to her old self...she admits that when the illness took over it was not an easy time..she had a rough time prior to her passing and she suffered in silence a great deal.. she was more concerned about what you and the family were going through than for herself...she does bless you for taking care of her, for being good to her prior to her passing...there was only so much you could do, and after a time your hands were tied...she wants you to know you could not have saved her.... she tried her best to get well, and you were certainly hoping also...but she tells me it was her time to pass on, as the individual that she is, and the illness was just the passport that took her where she was supposed to go

Your wife didn't believe in an afterlife?...she admits she was kind of on the fence.. she wasn't really sure deep down....not that she was an atheist by any means ...she was very spiritual but had uncertainties about what would happen next, like anybody, but has now found out there is an afterlife...

[this was a surprise, considering her apparent beliefs on earth, but perhaps she is just indicating she didn't realise that life would be so similar to earth, carrying on in bodily form etc]

You do pray for her in your own way? ...she thanks you for that, and she jokes that you are not a "holy roller"....you are spiritual in your own way but you had your uncertainties as well...she was on the fence but your were even more so...she believed in a more traditional way but you were the sceptic...she jokes that if she had not passed on you certainly wouldn't have been on the phone with the likes of me!

But her passing first has really broken the norm of your daily life and has put your world out of orbit, and that has made you think of other possibilities...your wife says again that you are no holy roller, nor should you consider becoming one...just be spiritual in a way that you are comfortable with...

[I had always spoken of going first, and had actually left Rachel a letter. The highly significant thing here also is that she is not telling me to go back to the EB or even to adopt any particular religion, which is quite a change from her earth time.]

She tells me she passed in a sleep state..in a coma or unconscious state...and this has nothing to do with any kind of organised religion or belief, what I'm about to say, it's just a comfort , that here in the room St Joseph appears...he is the patron of a happy death...it has nothing to do with being Catholic...he wasn't Catholic anyway. But to me he represents a happy death...so your wife is confirming her death was a peaceful one in spite of what led up to it.

She does tell me what she found enormously stressful with the illness was the loss of her independence...once the illness started depriving her of independence it was worse than the illness itself...because she was obviously a very independent , take-care-of-everyone type of person...she was the glue that held the family together...she knows she was the heart and soul of the home and the family...and that is another really frustrating part of your loss...losing the heart and soul of the home.

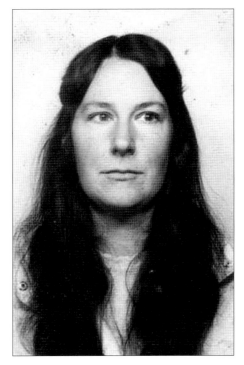

Above: Rachel, aged 18.

Below: July 1972, aged 19.
During a medium session she indicated that this is
her appearance now, in the spirit world.

Above: Christmas 1972.

Below: March 1973.

Above: Motherhood.

Below: In her late thirties.

Above and below: In Italy, a mere two years before her passing.

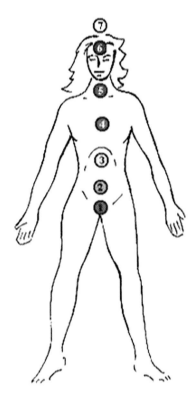

7. WHITE
Connecting us to Universal Consciousness.
Pituitary Gland.

6. VIOLET
Insight, intuition, clairvoyance, clairaudience,
clairsentience. 'Knowing' that is beyond words.
Pineal gland, third eye.

5. BLUE
Communication, responsibility, thyroid, rules
bodies timing and metabolism. Issues of timing.
Manifestation.

4. GREEN
Compassion, personal freedom, surrender,
forgiveness, acceptance. Gateway to higher Self.
Thymus helps to initiate immune system.

3. YELLOW
Mental issues, synthesis of ideas and feelings,
judgements and opinions. Childhood emotional
trauma, assimilation of sweetness, setting
boundaries, fear, ego.

2. ORANGE
Emotional issues, attachment and letting go of
people, places and things AS WELL AS ways of being.
Pyeres patches/Immune system center.

1. RED
Survival issues, anger, passion, lust, money,
career, shelter, pain, irritation.

The Seven Chakras

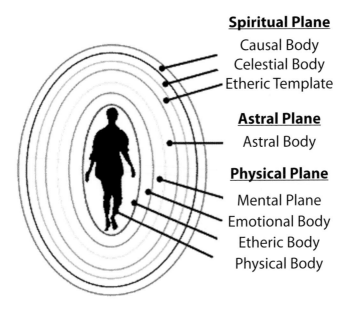

Spiritual Plane
Causal Body
Celestial Body
Etheric Template

Astral Plane
Astral Body

Physical Plane

Mental Plane
Emotional Body
Etheric Body
Physical Body

The Seven Bodies

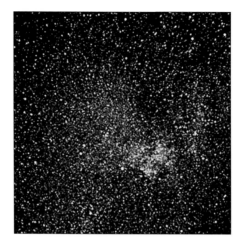

Above: …and we still fondly imagine that we are alone in the universe.
Below: We are connected to infinite energy.

Above: A colony of young stars in the Orion nebula… consciousness is creating every particle and sub-particle.

Below: The gods are watching us!

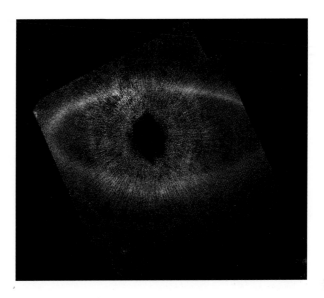

She knows and she does commend you for it, that you are trying to be the glue to keep it all together, but it is difficult ..she says...it IS more difficult to be a widower...but in her straightforward way she says...well...you do not have much of a choice...she knows you see it that way too...for the time being you know you have to put up with this...but she does hope you will feel comfortable going on with your life in whatever direction it takes you....that you will never have any issue with trying to be happy again and going on with your life, because, as your wife states, you have to...she says plainly that she will not think you don't love her any more if you try to be happy and go on with your life

She says again , you could not have saved her, you did not fail her..she knows you think you could have done more earlier....but she says she herself didn't know anything was wrong...she was tired but who goes to the doctor for that?

She tells me she had lower back pains...in the beginning it might have come and gone, but then it seemed to become more steadfast, so eventually she started thinking she had pulled a muscle or something. Who thinks that back pain is cancer? This illness did affect her lower abdominal region..she tells me the trouble starts there...and she says it was a form of cancer.....that is what she says , and now St Agatha appears to me, she is the patron of women with cancer, and that is a sign to me to confirm that she passed with cancer... in the lower abdominal region..it affected her private area....she also says you probably didn't notice that she was always thirsty and drinking a great deal of water...but she jokes that you aren't going to keep tabs on that...unless she had been drinking pints of beer or something!

[note: I checked with family and found the thirst thing to be correct. I had not known this]

She calls out to her own children...she doesn't want them to think she abandoned them

She goes back also...teasing you about being an agnostic....she says that before her passing you would have considered someone like me [the medium] as being "full of it"!

She says she comes to you in dreams..though you might not remember them...and she jokes that you feel you don't get enough signs from her...yet you talk to her all the time...and that is the sign...you talk to her because you instinctively know she is close...you sense her personality...and that is the sign you are overlooking...she says you are looking for something like a slab of concrete to hit you on the head...and that would be most uncomfortable! It doesn't happen that way so she says look at when you start talking to her without thinking, and that is her being very close to you.

She jokes also that your marriage had its ups and downs...but she hopes you agree that there were many more ups than downs....she says you were sometimes a tough nut to crack....but also admits there were times when she could be a tough nut to crack....in spite of all that, no matter what, you always loved each other, and still do.

She speaks the name Peter...there appears to be one on earth and one passed over...two Peters...but she does call out to the one on earth...Peter or Peeta... kidding around...so I presume you know who that is...they don't always explain ...but it comes to YOU in a manner you understand

["Peeta" is the way she pronounced Peter, with her English accent, and was always a little private joke between us. As regards the other Peter we will see later in the book that we don't bring all our energy to earth --we leave some of it in the spirit world. Or of course there might be another Peter I don't know about]

Also the name Anne or Anna
[Anne is a daughter, as is Diana]

Someone here not expecting to be recognised, called Alice , who is with your wife
[Speculate that this is the still-born daughter, as Alice is a name in the family]

Also Kathy , or Katy, some K sound, and Henry or Harry
[Possibly meant to be Karen, another daughter. Henry or Harry is not known at this time]

Your wife says you have moved house...she knows you are trying to move on and don't have much of a choice.. but she goes with you
[at this point the medium got it wrong, saying I was about to move house, and I just let it go. However, in a couple of minutes he said my wife had corrected him, saying I had already moved]
She thanks you for the memorial
She speaks of there being a great joyful reunion for her when she passed on, with people and animals from the course of her life
[the animal reference was a surprise to me at the time, but very much a possibility]

She speaks again of being able to walk fine and being back to her old self...that message must mean something deep to you even though it sounds mundane to me...and she is in a happy place , having a well-earned holiday
[She had lost the power of her legs during her illness. For me this not only made sense but raised the question about the whole idea of the resurrection

that people supposedly await at the end of time. Rachel is apparently already in her new body, not asleep in some great limbo awaiting "the resurrection of the dead".]

I am puzzled by this...it sounds like Irene or Eileen...your wife is saying the name but it sounds like it is at the end of a tunnel...like static on the radio sometimes....she says she is with Irene ....and now Irene is calling out to YOU as well

[Irene was my sister who died as a child, a year before I was born, so even I hadn't known her.]

She speaks of the loss of a child too...before birth...there with her now....she was confusing me earlier with talk of a child and children....I wondered which it could be...she obviously knew you would understand....child over there... children still on earth
She speaks of a son, and sends him white roses in congratulations

[her son was hooking up with his future wife at this time, not known about by us before Rachel passed]

She says that when she passed over her daughter over there was one of the first souls to welcome her, and even though she never knew her, a mother always knows her children, and they are together...also the daughter calls out to her siblings on earth
I hear a name that sounds like Jane

[speculate Elaine, another daughter]

Also Maureen
[My mother]

She speaks of a white-lace celebration up ahead in the family, and again extends white roses in congratulation...one of her children getting married... she says she will be there spiritually...you wish she would be there physically but it is the best she can do.....also speaks of a happy birth, but that could be five years or more
[marriage of daughter Anne, again not on the cards before Rachel passed]

Now she is pulling back...she repeats that it was her time to pass on...as part of her spiritual journey...she assures you that when your time comes, she will welcome you over, just as her daughter welcomed her over, so you and your wife will hook up again...she jokes that you have to show up there sometime... she embraces YOU with love and sends love to her children, son and daughters, and your daughter does the same from there, and your mother-in-law and your dad and all the others...but it's obvious who you really wanted to hear from. Your dad made the connection and your wife then came forward immediately. She wants you to know she is at peace and in a happy place. Try to put yourself in a happy place. Know that she is always with you in a loving way.

This is the main thrust of what came through. Some very personal and private references are omitted.

So, does that sound demonic? My wife sends me loving thoughts and comforting evidence of her continued existence. What would a demon achieve by doing that?

I concluded from this, beyond any personal doubt, that Rachel was alive and well in another dimension of life. She had not only described past events, including exact details of her illness, but showed me that she was aware of my life at present, and her humour and unique personality, so well known and loved by me, came through. I had not really expected any other relatives to come through but there was my father, my sister, and a still-born baby daughter that we had had in 1980. As stated earlier, my previous belief was that a still-born child was just a failed pregnancy, so it was a surprise to find she was a real person. In several sessions with different mediums over the next four years Rachel never failed to come through and the information she gave just confirmed to me the reality of life continuing after death in a vibrant, fully alive kind of way, not in some cloudy limbo awaiting resurrection and judgment. I had an awful lot more to learn about how life develops in other dimensions, and still have, but this information was enough to change my life in the meantime.

I was fascinated and I became obsessed with searching for ever more evidence. George Anderson had been brought up in the Roman Catholic tradition and he still uses some of that imagery, referring to the presence of certain figures in terms of traditionally known Christian saints. Yet in one of his books he describes doing a tour of Japan and in his sessions there those **very same figures** were appearing as icons of the Shinto religion. Great figures of Light who serve and help us are not bothered about how they are perceived or named.

Accepting that life is eternal, means it exists as a continuum outside of time and space as we know it, yet we experience real time on earth as part of our existence that has no beginning and no end. Each personality of earth life is a new creation that lives on and develops in dimensions we hardly comprehend. In truth the more I found out the more it all made sense. In some religions it is believed that we progress to eventual re-absorption into the Source, or a Nirvana where we merge into a kind of formless anonymity. The EB in particular were very much against natural family relations "intruding" into spiritual life even on earth, never mind the idea of them continuing beyond death. Their current tombstones each list only the name of the deceased and the date of death, with no mention of any family link. To them the family link does not carry forward into "heaven", though they tend to be vague about what does happen. I was beginning to learn that each personality retains its uniqueness and carries on life much as before only with greater freedom and at a higher level. Rachel came through identifying herself as my sweetheart, saying that she would always be my sweetheart. Yet she told me to go on and find someone else because this would not mean to her that I didn't love her any more. I realised that outside of time it would be possible to have multiple sweethearts, each of them one hundred per cent in love. Perhaps that love in itself would evolve into something much greater than our current understanding, yet not leaving anything behind. If there is no time, you can't leave anything behind. Everything just IS. Our earth time dictates that we follow a linear pattern, doing one thing at a time, but step outside time and consciousness expands its abilities. Simultaneous is a word that comes close but doesn't even describe it accurately, as that is still a time-related term.

I researched many other psychic mediums, in particular the direct voice medium Leslie Flint who had served to bring through thousands of souls for around 50 years up until his death in the nineties. There are recordings of hours and hours of communications from some well-known people and some unknown people in all walks of life. These are now available on the internet at www.leslieflint.com. The significant thing here again is that the personality goes on. There is broad agreement on the nature of life in the hereafter, but also many variations. Sceptics will point to the variations as proof that it is mere imagination, but what we have to realise is that each personality is describing his or her own unique experience. Just as on earth we each see the world in our own way, so in another dimension we do the same. Those who have led very religious lives on earth may continue to see things in those same terms when they pass over, although some may awaken rather more quickly to a wider reality. You do not automatically awaken to some great absolute truth that is handed to you on a plate. You continue to learn by experience and by expanding your consciousness, and you do so at your own pace. Your experience will also be affected by how much you learned in previous lives. Many religious people may actually group together in that afterlife situation, creating and perpetuating their idea of heaven for quite a long time in earth terms. Some diehard atheists may remain inert or unconscious for long periods of earth time simply because they refuse to believe that life goes on. Advanced souls who have gone through the experiences themselves over aeons of earth time are always working to enlighten and rescue souls who are in darkness due to their beliefs.

Less than eighteen months later, despite all my efforts to move on, I was relapsing into despair and I booked another session with George Anderson. The main part of the session is given here to show just how detailed and how personal was the information that came through. At this point I had returned to relying too much on whiskey to blot out my distress, and although not quite suicidal, I usually went to bed at night hoping I wouldn't wake up again, and on some days I would drive really recklessly in the vague hope of wiping myself out in an accident.

As before, no help was given by me and no help was asked for by the medium. Readers obviously only have my word for the experience, although it was recorded, but why would I invent such a thing anyway? Some comments are interspersed:

A female comes forward, actually 3, there's two more with her and a couple of males in the background as well, but the first female draws very close to YOU, so she must be somebody close to you...she says she does come to you in dreams.

Now she does come to you as your wife...she comes as your sweetheart in a romantic sense, and in this case as your wife...and not that she is trying to add salt to the wound, but she says you still have that wish that you had gone before her, or at least you had gone together. But she says, Not yet!

She is assuring you that when the time comes, when you are supposed to go, that she will certainly come for you and she will welcome you over, and she knows that is a day you look forward to...that's OK, but you are NOT supposed to be there yet!

So she says, kind of kidding you, don't, so to speak, as they say, storm the gates of heaven...not that she is being religious or anything, but she sort of gets a kick out of the fact that you are trying to rush the deal.

She says you are dealing with it as best you can, and she is proud of that, but she knows that in the back of your mind you are trying to rush it and get it over with. But she says that will only make it seem longer and more difficult. She knows it is difficult enough as it is, but don't add fuel to the fire.

She knows that as long as you know that when the time comes for you she will be there to welcome you, that it does make it a bit easier, but even so you just have to wait until it is your time. She says she is your sweetheart and always will be, but you are still your own person on your own journey, and as much as you may feel at this point, especially since she passed on, that you are finished.....you feel you are done....but apparently, she says, you are not done, otherwise you would be out of here!

So if you can just for a moment detach yourself from her and see yourself as your own person on your own journey, she hopes that you will realise that's why you haven't crossed the threshold yet . But she knows it is understandable, you spent a nice life together, and even though you have family and such, you still feel a little like you're finished.

But your wife seems to be the type of lady who tells it straightforward, and she repeats that you are not supposed to be there yet...she is not being unkind to you or insensitive to your feelings, she is just being herself and letting you know.

She speaks also of her children.

She does remark that you could take better care of yourself....you are not about, as YOU might say UNFORTUNATELY, you are not about to drop dead tomorrow, but she does tell me you are out of balance with yourself.

Make sure you are eating right, getting enough rest, not going to extremes. She realises there is a part of you that doesn't give a you-know-what since she has passed on...at times you are playing Russian Roulette with your life...like.. who cares ...what's the worst that can happen...she says that is only adding to the already apparent frustration...because you are not going to be over there unless you are supposed to be.

She does tell you to watch what goes in your mouth, so that could be to watch what you're eating or drinking...that you don't go to extremes

That is what she is driving at, too much is just as bad as too little.. I don't want to jump to conclusions...but she is telling you to watch your drinking...... she is not saying you are a rip-roaring alcoholic....but at times you are kind of trying to ease your sorrows...she says you are turning to it to kind of take the bite off... not that there is anything wrong with that...she is not judging you on it...she knows it does make things a bit easier....like taking medication to take the edge off the pain...but she says just be careful that are not going to an extreme or a dependency.

She knows that sadly each day you feel you are walking in a circle, like a dog chasing its tail, you are not going anywhere.

Your wife realises and she is not saying this out of conceit, that when on earth she was unquestionably the heart and soul of the home....not that you were some flunkey in it, but you would even agree with her on that. She was the glue that kept everything together, plus she knows that you have lost your best friend as well as your sweetheart...you miss her company as much as anything. She knows that.. and she knows that sometimes you've even been mistaken... she is kidding you in a pleasant way...when you've spoken or done something and then realised she's not there physically any more.

She says she is around you very much as a guardian angel...but she also says that you must understand that she can't fix your life, nor lead you around by the nose. She says, I 'm not your fairy godmother over here who can wave a magic wand and make everything go the way you want it.

This is a temporary separation of form..that is all it is..and she says eventually you have to show up over there, but only when the time is right. She says that dealing with her loss is part of your spiritual journey...you are still in that part of it...so try your best to go with the flow.

She is concerned that you are isolating yourself from family and friends... keeping to yourself....and struggling with depression.

She says that if you are struggling with depression and it is getting out of control, you should not try to tough it out on your own...don't be embarrassed or ashamed to seek therapeutic help. She knows you feel dreadfully empty inside ,and she understands that, but she says keep in mind that depression is an illness and after a time it can snowball and get worse.

She is not suggesting you are ready for the looney bin....just don't suffer in silence.

You try not to get in anybody's way, and you maintain your independence. She says that on a bad day you you don't want people fussing over you just because you are the poor widower or something... she jokes that you can be a hard nut to crack sometimes! She says jokingly to you, there is a right way and a wrong way, and then there's YOUR way.

She is very concerned that presently you seem to be at a crossroads, kind of stuck, neither here nor there...she is concerned about that...because if you feel trapped emotionally, feel emptiness, and a sense of being closed in, it becomes very difficult....you are the one pulling back, going into your own world so to speak....she knows your main point is to not get in anybody's hair, not to become dependent on anybody...that's fine...

But the more you keep to yourself the more you think too much....and thinking is a great thing...but too much is as bad as too little...and dangerous when you brood over your failings and whatever...she is trying to help you to help yourself from where she is...but ultimately the task has to be accomplished by you...you are in control of your own life.

She knows that recently you have gone through stages where you wish you would just die...get it over with...wishing you wouldn't wake up in the morning, at least not on earth anyway, but that is just a frustrating struggle.

She says that grief has turned your world upside down...but you are not a vulnerable person...you are NOT a stupid person, so you know yourself what is the common sense thing to do. She says you are creating demons in your life, not in a religious sense, and they don't actually exist.

She would like you to get focused in another direction...she can't break your arm to make you do it...to get focussed and distracted....because when you have too much time to think...you brood.

She says if you go on with life she is not going to take that as meaning you don't love her any more, or you are being disrespectful to her memory or to her person. She wants you to be happy and to go on with your life, and that will make things seem a great deal faster...though each day seems like an eternity yet each day is one step nearer, one day less...till you meet again.

Also she says that when this session is over you must not start brooding and reading between the lines...don't do that..she is NOT criticising you or telling you that you are a failure or anything of the kind so don't think that. She knows you are in a very sensitive state of mind right now, where she is concerned you could think about what she has said and then put your own words into it....she is not criticising you, just trying to help you to help yourself to fulfil this part of your journey.

I'm hearing others also, she is not alone....sounds like Alice? Your wife says she is with her over there and they are very close, and close to you.

[Probably the daughter who was still-born]

Also heard the name George....he calls out to you, he is in the crowd that is there with your wife. He reaches out to you and he and the others want you to know that you are not alone....because that is one thing they and your wife recognise...that you feel a terrible sense of emptiness and aloneness, of being left behind...they want to assure you that they are around you....it may not be the best compensation you would like , but it is better than nothing and the best they can do.

[George is my father]

Up until your wife's passing you didn't believe in a hereafter? Prior to her passing you just thought well, I'll find out when I die...but now you know there is life afterwards. She refers to your religious background and gives an impression that it is just not there for you.

[I think this an interesting reference to the EB]

She refers to a white lace celebration up ahead and she calls out to her children, nobody to be left out...

She says it was definitely her time to pass on and you could not have changed that......again she is on about you thinking too much...you keep going over her passing and over your life and blaming yourself for all your so-called failures... and she says you are just making it worse than it really is. So she wants you to stop doing that...and then when you drink too much you brood and reflect too *much and you drown yourself in your own sorrow.*

Don't be so hard-nosed that you tough it all out on your own in silence...she says that any time you feel the depths of depression...while she can't cure it...she does draw very close to you. She is closer to you than you can imagine.

She calls out again to her children and mentions a child over there with her also.

She just ASSURES you that you are not alone....she knows that is the most struggling emotion you are dealing with...and you tough it out by yourself, making it worse....she really does stay close to you.

I thought I heard the name Carol, Katy, Kathy...
[probably Karen , her daughter]
Also Isobel who says you might not know her..
Julie or Julia..
[still not known]

Anyway it's obvious you really just wanted to hear from your wife....the others too of course, but your main focus is on your wife.

Also Diane or Diana...somebody still on earth...she sends white roses to her in congratulations
[her daughter Diana had recently completed a parachute jump for charity]

Doris...
[not known]

Your wife writes the word Gloria in front of me , and then Grace. Gloria symbolises happy news...something up ahead for the family.

Your wife jokes that you pray for her in your own way....she says it wouldn't have been your cup of tea before she passed over...she thanks you for it...she is not a holy roller, nor has she become one...and you haven't become one either... but it gives you a way to do something positive for her and to embrace her with your love, and she wants you to know she is aware of that.

Also Irene or Eileen..
[As already mentioned, Irene is my sister who died a year before I was born, and so would no doubt have followed my life closely]

She must be close to your wife because I have been hearing her since the beginning of the session. Your wife is saying that Irene is with her, and Irene herself also calls out to you. Your wife says Irene and her have become great friends over there....which is nice to hear...even if they didn't know each other on earth..or whatever...your wife is getting impatient with me again...she says it doesn't matter if they knew each other or not they are good friends now!

Also Arthur...says you might not recognise him
Emily....
[couldn't place them at this point, but I later realised that they are Rachel's grandparents]

Jane...
[not known, but maybe the sound of Elaine, another daughter]

Your wife says she has met many new friends also since she passed over and you might not know some of them
The name Peter...she doesn't explain....
She says she wants you to know she is fine and back to her old self again...she speaks of the health troubles that took her over....but she doesn't want to rehash that....she is back to her old self and she wants to help you to get back to your old self....and to get you into a safe place emotionally. She says she knows you love her, and she certainly loves you, but she is in a happy safe place over there. She knows that in many respects you are not in a safe place with yourself, and that is why she is trying to help you

The Jane sound again...and Betty or Eddie.....your wife calling the names.
[Elaine, and Debbie are daughters]

She is pulling back now...this has been quite unusual as a session......but she says she wanted to focus the session on YOU and your emotional state....that was her concern...not to rehash old news and stuff....just focusing on you and your state of being...mental and emotional....and she doesn't think you are a wacko or anything...she is just trying to bring you peace of mind by letting you know she sees what you go through and she is trying to help you help yourself. She certainly does embrace you with love, and her children also. All the crowd of souls there with her are calling out to you also, but everybody knows who you most wanted to hear from. She embraces you and urges you to think about what she has said. She can't wave a magic wand...the rest is up to you. But even after this transition we call death she assures you that she will always be helping you in any way she can. Try to get yourself back into balance and know that she is always close to you.

There are many other verifiable details that came through in other sessions with different mediums and the following are just some examples. It is not possible to list everything, as some details are very personal. The material included in this book is much less than half of all I have experienced in medium sessions. All of the communication to me has been really subtle, detailed and vibrantly alive. There has never been any attempt at fishing or mind-reading. I have no doubt that some mediums are better than others, and every medium to some extent colours the communication as it filters through their own mind. Some mediums have a belief in dark forces and they will therefore misinterpret what they are sensing.It is important to be discerning and to concentrate on the fact that you are in touch with your loved ones, the medium being just a conduit.

*Rachel thanked me for the roses, which I had just days previously put on her grave for a private reason that would be unknown to anyone else.

*My mother-in-law came through to comment on her previous dislike of me while on earth, and to set things straight in quite a lot of detail. This is not something I would make up!

*Rachel commented on the surprisingly large number at her funeral.

*More than once, different mediums described her appearance accurately, including her distinctive hair and eyes and figure.

*Rachel described her deathbed scene with total accuracy, even though she had been unconscious at the time.

*Rachel said she is now dancing and painting, two things which I personally know she always secretly wanted to do on earth, but felt constrained by her religious qualms.She also said she wished she could convey how extraordinary the music is over there.

*Rachel said she had met two of the people from the hospital ward where she had been admitted first. [This is significant: in her first hospitalisation she was fussing over some of the other patients who were unable to help themselves at that stage. It seems acts of kindness are very much remembered].

*Rachel said she had met her sisters, [the twins who died before she was born, one still-born and one who lived briefly]

*In one session my father and Rachel went over very detailed family history, with others, showing how they were now working through various issues from their earth life. No one could have guessed at that material, and it could not have been mind-reading either

*In another session Rachel described in startling detail what I had been doing and thinking for the hour previous to the session, when I was walking around to kill time before the appointment.

* In 2008 I was in Palm Springs, California, on a week's training course. Afterwards I drove across the desert for five hours to Tucson in Arizona

to visit good friends, Jack Andrews and Susan Anway. They lived out in the desert with giant Saguaro cacti and rattlesnakes for company. They are not mediums but are very sensitive to spiritual realities. Just hours before I arrived they both had separate manifestations from Rachel. They had never met her or even seen photos of her, yet they described aspects of her character and mannerisms that were uncannily accurate.

*Rachel recently expressed regret that she had refused to open her mind to other religions and other ideas while on earth.

Some sceptics point triumphantly to apparent mistakes and difficulties in the communications. Those passed over are supposed to be supermen and superwomen who know everything, and should be able to contact us with perfect ease if they are real at all. The fact is that communication is difficult from their side as well as ours, and in some cases is even affected by the physical atmosphere. People talk about psychic ability as if it is magic or supernatural. It is in fact part of our natural make-up. As with all gifts, some people have it more intensely than others, but it is part of human nature to be in touch with the spirit world, since, for one obvious reason, that is where we come from in the first place. Indeed the realms of the newly "dead" are most probably on or close to earth rather than light years away. Psychic ability does not equate with goodness or piety either. It is purely a human attribute, and if sceptics would take time to ponder this they would not get themselves so confused. There is no distinct boundary to any part of the universe.

I am not suggesting that everybody should contact a medium. It is possible to become addicted to it in a way that would not be helpful. Yet it is clear that certain people have been available throughout history as living bridges between earth and the spirit world. This is not accidental, and the opportunity exists for contact for anyone who chooses. So far, I have tried to have a specific purpose for contact, and Rachel and the others appear happy to cooperate. On one occasion I was anxious in my mind that maybe I was being a nuisance; I did not say it aloud, yet the first words that came through were, "your wife says she really doesn't mind you coming like this". There will probably come a time when I no longer feel it is necessary. I do not believe, however, that there are any rules about it; no one in the spirit world is forbidding the practice; indeed they appear very keen to help us, and it is part of their ongoing purpose. The most likely reason for banning it is once again the need for religious authorities to control people's lives and beliefs. Getting a clearer picture of who we are and where we come from rather undermines the authority of church and priest. It also totally undermines the scientific attempts to deny that life goes on, so those naysayers focus exclusively on the charlatans and pretend that real mediums do not exist. Love, however, is the greatest force that exists. It is unbreakable and it cannot be limited. Follow the desires of pure love and you will not go wrong. The spirits of departed loved ones are not "called up"; they are aware of the appointment with the medium and they come through voluntarily and with love. You are not disturbing their rest; they are more fully alive than you are. If you are asking them to run your life they will tell you that you need to run your own life, but they are always ready to help you.

I will quote one extract from one of the sessions from Leslie Flint. This is a communication from someone named George Briggs, and is freely available in full on the website.

"...in my own narrow way when I was on your side I sincerely believed at the time that only those who accepted and believed as I did, would inherit the Kingdom of God. I know this is a fallacy now--that all peoples inherit the Kingdom of God because it is a natural law. No one is barred, no one is kept out, for the simple reason that it is natural law that when man dies his spirit inherits the spiritual realms which are all around and about your earth world. It is inescapable..."

Almost five years after Rachel's passing I recorded another session with a local medium. Rachel's father had now passed away since I had the previous contact. As I mentioned before, Rachel's mother had more than once come through with the message that though she had disliked me on earth she had now changed her mind. In one session she admitted that she had never thought I was good enough for Rachel, and after that she has always made an appearance when I have visited a medium. It is quite a change for me to be friends with my in-laws, and it is a wonderful example of how we progress, if not here, then later on. In this session, the main points quoted below, she was actually the first to come through, with her husband also, and it is apparent that they have worked out their issues from their earth life:

Right..the first contact is from a mother figure...your mother-in-law...there is a father figure here also...but I will concentrate on your mother-in-law first... she says she lost children also, who are now with her in the spirit world....and she is talking about her husband who died with cancer now being with her... the two of them come forward here to you...they also mention a John who is there too....your father-in-law wants to show me that he was a man who didn't always show his emotions...he is saying he was a man who didn't get on with everybody in many ways....in some ways he could, but he is a complex character...and he has a daughter there with him...this lady also died with cancer...but a different type of cancer to her father's....this is your wife....she is mentioning someone called Mary there with her....

Note: some of the problems with the in-laws were personal as described before, but some of it would be to do with the EB background also.

Mary is Rachel's aunt, who was always a much more balanced individual than her sister.

your wife says she really wanted to pass away at home, but the cancer got so advanced that it wasn't really possible...she also mentions Anne.....so what we have really is your wife coming through with her parents.....can you understand that your sweet wife is saying that maybe her parents were a bit odd?...and she would have had her problems with them too...it wasn't all a walk in the park...it wasn't happy...but they have sorted it out now...she says they were a bit dysfunctional....she is speaking again of Mary who would be older than her... and Mary also knew you...she is a very down to earth decent likeable type who would take to anybody....

Note; as above, and her Aunt Mary was often a help to Rachel when her mother was being strange.

your wife is saying she lived with the cancer without knowing it...until it was too late to do anything....she is saying she suffered a bloating up like she had never had....and that was very uncomfortable and annoying in her illness.... and it depressed her...now your wife wants to show me that she lost a child too...

...now about her father....she is saying he could be quite an odd man...he would do strange things...he estranged himself from people too...he was a complicated character and you could never quite get to him...her mother was different...but her mother had her own quirks too....but in a different way... there was a certain set of problems with her father and another set of problems with her mother...and your wife says that between her and her mother there was not a very brilliant bridge...they were mother and daughter but very very different in their ways...her mother could have manipulated people quite a lot....she was Mrs Manipulator....but your wife would not have stooped to that sort of thing...it wasn't her way...and she used to get very very annoyed with her mother....her mother with her attitude didn't do herself any favours....the good thing is that they have resolved it all over there...but there seems to be an apology going towards your wife....her parents apologising to her....it doesn't need to be the other way round...because their behaviour to her left her with many unhappy memories.....and your wife certainly didn't want any of that sort of thing repeating in your life together...she is not saying she was perfect in any way....but she carried a set of problems from her parents...of which her parents are now admitting to honestly and they have made their peace...

she is saying she didn't want to be so heavily medicated at the end...it spaced her out

Note: with hindsight it would have been better to have less medication, so that Rachel could stay conscious, but at the time we just wanted her to be free of pain.

...now she is showing me your father....he has been in the spirit world a lot longer than them...he mentions a Willie over there on his side of the family... and a Bobbie....who passed with cancer too....your father went more suddenly he says but there was illness too...and lost a lot of weight....and there was also difficulty around his chest area and his breathing was affected....he is saying, not comparing it to your in-laws, but his family could have been a bit strange too...and they weren't connected to you

Note: I did not know of my father's illness or death until after he was buried, due to him being back with the EB. Ref his family they were always estranged from us when we were growing up, because we were EB and they were not. This was more our fault than theirs.

...your father is talking about a female here on earth with blood pressure problems...your mother....he sees that she is being cared for and he wants you to know it is very much appreciated from their side...and her mother, your grandmother, is there and she seems to feel you would have known her side of the family better

My maternal grandparents were EB so we did know them better

....your wife says her life here had a definite purpose to it....and while she was here she was a person who would like to keep people together....she wouldn't cause people to break up...and she didn't like being out at elbows with people... that is why she is so glad to get closure with her parents now....because it never happened down here

...she says she was really torn about leaving you and the family....it was not an easy decision...she really loved the life with you all...but she is very happy and contented over there now...but she says she has a massively strong connection to YOU...and she knows you sense her presence with you even though it is not physical

...your father is speaking about your mother....and quite honestly they just didn't get on...he says he knows that wasn't a good marriage...there wasn't much happiness there...a lot of misery...they were like two magnets that oppose each other...and putting them together was just too much...they pushed each other away...and at some stage they separated...but he does feel he could have been more patient from his side ...and he regrets really running away and making a new life...because he pulled away from you...went and invented another life...he does come over with respect for her, but he knows it wasn't the ideal marriage....and he can't say more than that...he was never a man to really face

up to his troubles...he would love you to know something though, and that is that you have approached life differently, and you are a different person....he apologises to you because his attitude to you wasn't helpful...but he says you managed to by-pass his mistakes ...he says you are made of better stuff... he says you have an honesty and an integrity and a down-to-earth-ness and a connectedness that he lacked...he says there was part of him that never grew up....and he is not copping out but maybe his own upbringing didn't help....now your wife is here smiling ...because she is glad to see you two sorting all this out and knows you are glad to hear this...it was unfinished business...although they know you had let go of all the anger long ago anyway

Note: Rachel was always aware of how much I loved my father, and how the whole separation business really tormented me. This is also typical of her desires to see people resolving their differences.

Part of her problem in letting go of the EB was related to this horror of falling out with people.

...now your father is saying that he knows some people were not at his funeral...but he understands why that happened

Note: as mentioned before we did not even know he was dead until after his funeral.

...anyway he sends you his love and he owns to all his mistakes

...and your wife sends her love, she is in a happy place....she is close to you.... she says you brought out the best in each other

....your mum's mum is there ...and she mentions a Sally also....and once again thanks you all for taking care of mum.

I know that all involved here are happy for this to be part of the story. I asked them to give me some material for the book and this is what they gave. It simply illustrates how every earth experience can lead to development of the soul, and what we miss out on in earth we catch up with eventually. I am not pretending that I was better than any of them, and for myself I still have the rest of my earth road to travel. It shows too the importance of not judging others. We really are acting in our own drama in life and we attract all the experiences that happen to us and all the people who enter our lives. I needed the lessons they taught me, and they needed the lessons I taught them. There is no real need for apologies as such, but it is nice to arrive at closure on these matters. Later in the book we will see that the earth ego or personality is not extinguished when we pass on, but at the same time it is not the whole story. Each life we live on earth, each personality created, is a part of a greater higher self or oversoul and goes on to contribute to that entity. Some of our incarnations on earth will be more "successful" than others but every set of experiences contributes to the expanding consciousness of who we truly are.

CHAPTER 14
Near Death Experiences

It was quite a surprise to me when I was searching that there was such a vast amount of evidence to show that life does go on in other dimensions. Perhaps the internet has brought much more to our attention. Previously if bookshops did not stock such material we just remained in ignorance, and the media generally are only interested in the subject in a superficial way. It is customary to hear people repeating mantras like "we'll never know", "nobody ever came back and described it", "it's too spooky", "there is no evidence of a God" etc etc. But yes, life goes on, thousands of people have described it, it is not in the least bit spooky, and we can know a great deal about it right now. Remembering from years past Raymond Moody's book on near-death-experiences, "Life after Life", I read it again. It is interesting to quote from the preface of the later edition, written by Melvin Morse, another researcher in the same field:

"When Dr Moody's book was first published medical science laughed and dismissed near-death experiences as hallucinations. Twenty-five years later, science is on Dr Moody's side. I do not know of a single mainstream scientific researcher who has not reached similar conclusions. There have been three major reviews of near-death experiences in the scientific literature of the past seven years, and all agree with Dr Moody's findings..."

Because of the scepticism around the experiences with psychic mediums, I wanted to look at the subject from as many viewpoints as possible, though I personally had no doubts. It seems to me that if I can see the same patterns emerging from different sources it is much harder for sceptics to dismiss it. Much serious research is still being done in this area, and the evidence is very strong that consciousness can leave the body and return to it. Consciousness is focused in flesh for its time on earth but it does not depend on flesh for its existence. The brain is the transmitter for the mind, but the mind exists outside of it. A blind person could see when out of body, being able to describe the doctors that had worked on his body, yet was blind again when he returned to it. A woman described in detail a shoe that was on the window sill of a hospital's fifth floor that she could only have seen from the outside. The shoe was found and the details were exact. Hundreds of stories have been carefully gathered and recorded. A man who almost drowned was aware of rising out of his body and sharing consciousness with the trees and the landscape. The idea that it is all hallucination due to oxygen deprivation simply does not answer more than a tiny fraction of the cases. The reader is urged to do the research before rejecting the evidence out of hand. There are similar stories told in antiquity by Plato and others. For my part, I remember that Rachel described the state of our garden at home during the last days of her illness when she was bodily in the hospice and incapable of having seen it. Yet she was accurately describing its present condition, which was one of neglect due to the crisis, and she was expressing disappointment. Also, the house opposite to ours had a rare orchid or some such flower which blossomed very briefly each year, and she noted that this was in bloom.

There are thousands of experiences recorded, and the sources are once again listed at the end of the book. Most people have beautiful experiences of the spirit world, but some do have frightening ones. The overwhelming evidence from a study of all the sources included in this book and elsewhere will show that demons and devils are created by the mind of the perceiver, through fear in the conscious mind, and are not real beings. I cannot prove this, but I have arrived at my views by studying it from many different angles and seeing the overall pattern. There is the evidence of the psychic mediums, plus these near-death-experiences. Later I will discuss the hypnotic regressions, which are the descriptions of past lives, past deaths, and lives between lives. Then there are the out-of-body projections, described extensively by Robert Monroe. There is also the entity called Ramtha, who channelled through a lady called J Z Knight. Then there is the entity called Seth, who channelled through the writer and mystic Jane Roberts. There are so many sources and the reader who is serious about soul development really needs to search out what is there, keeping an open mind. For quite a long time in my life I was one who would dismiss all this without giving it a second thought. There was no greater sceptic than I was and I would have been amazed to see my future self writing this book.

Michael Sabom's book, "Light and Death" describes the case of a patient who was undergoing major daring surgery to remove an aneurysm in her head. The details of the surgery are certainly not for the squeamish; the point is that she was flat-lining, brain dead for more than half an hour. Yet afterwards she was able to recount that she could see, hear and feel what was going on from a point "sitting" on the surgeon's shoulder. As well as that she moved through a tunnel and met several deceased relatives. While bathed in an incredible, ineffable light she communicated telepathically with them, but was told not to advance any further, and her deceased uncle accompanied her back to her body. She really didn't want to rejoin her body, but she was gently made to do so as it was not her time to leave.

One of the most famous and startling experiences was that of Mellen-Thomas Benedict: this man was dying of cancer and was somehow able to go consciously into the experience, which opened up into unimaginable realms, from the Big Bang to four hundred years into the future. His journey took him past stars and galaxies to an overview of all worlds and and all creation. He saw all wars; he saw races as personality clusters, species operating like cells in a greater whole; he saw planetary energy systems in detail and how human thoughts influence these systems in an interplay between past, present and future. He learned that earth is a great cosmic being. When after ninety minutes he fell back into his body, the cancer that was killing him had vanished. The full experience is once again freely available on the internet.

In "Mindsight", by Kenneth Ring and Sharon Cooper, they study the near-death-experiences of blind people. All the subjects say that in their ordinary dreams they do not have visual perception. Yet during their out-of-body experience they do have visual perception, and on return to ordinary consciousness they are blind again. There are arguments about whether these people are really "seeing" or whether it is some other kind of awareness. I would think it is obvious that it is another type of awareness-- the consciousness is outside of the body and is not depending on the physical eyes or any of the five senses at all. Thus people even describe 360 degree vision and awareness of exactly how many hairs there are on someone's head. The human body is extremely limited compared to its spiritual counterpart. Reports from the other side often speak of the sheer joy of leaving behind a body so limited in its capabilities.

A common theme that runs through each experience is the Light, which is warm and peaceful and non-judgmental. It is alive and personal, knowing, and it embraces you wholly. It is a not a person in the sense or form that we are used to, but it is definitely far more than an impersonal force of energy. It is instinctively recognisable to many as the Source and Substance of all things and all people. In the presence of this Light you can receive the answers to every question you can ask, instantly, without words. You can experience an infinitely greater range of music and colour and beauty far above the very best this earth can offer. That is not to minimise the great beauty of earth by any means, but to show its source. It would seem that everything we create on earth is an extension into denser matter of what has already been. Evolution is the intelligent creative tool that consciously brings more and more Light and Beauty into physical manifestation.

Those who experience being in the presence of this Light do not feel fear or unworthiness. They feel themselves embraced with incredible love; they feel at home; they feel connected to all that is. The heart responds to this Being of Light with joy and delight. Though the Light is essentially formless it can and does display any form it chooses.

It is argued by some, with justification, that near-death is not actual death. This does not take away from its evidential quality. Cortez saw the Pacific from a mountain top; Moses was shown the Promised Land; we can all see the stars at night though we haven't been there, at least in this lifetime. We will see later in the Seth writings that the cosmos is full of different systems of reality. In this case, say, we know that our physical life is one system of reality with its own rules and values. The other system we are looking at is very close to us, the one to which we go immediately after this one. Seth says that in all the myriad systems of reality that exist, while there are obvious boundaries to them, none of them are sealed off completely. In theory all systems are accessible in some way to every other one. Thus in our study here we can accept that communication between these very close systems does take place. In Heading Towards Omega, Kenneth Ring goes on to document the profound effects these experiences have had on individual lives. A person out of body can certainly at least glimpse the spirit world even if they haven't entered it in the same full way as someone who has actually died, and it is usually a life-changing event.

It can be difficult for us on earth to grasp that Life just IS; it cannot "NOT BE". There is no beginning to life and there is no end to life. There is a beginning and an end to your physical body, but think carefully--what is that force you call life which makes itself known in a newborn baby and then leaves that body many years later? Where does it come from and where does it go? You cannot deny its existence. I have known in my experience what a still-born child is; and I have known what six live children are. I have seen my wife's body in life and at the moment of its death. My wife did not die, though her body did. There is a spirit that animates the body when any of us are physically alive; we know that and we see it eventually leaving again. In terms of our physical existence it must come in the first place from outside of that body, and it must move on to somewhere else outside of that body at so-called death. Energy cannot be destroyed. **Something that has no beginning has no end.** Despite the sneers of those who deny the afterlife, it is they who are being naive, and I am embarrassed that I was once almost among their number. Yet it is not my place to judge or condemn anyone else for their beliefs; I am responsible for myself.

It would really be better if we didn't use the word "afterlife", as it is misleading. It tends to suggest that we live one life on earth and then there is another one afterwards. The bible states that it is appointed unto man "once to die and after that the judgment" [Hebrews 9:27], but the reality is so much greater than that. Someone may have added that comment in the bible afterwards for all we know, or the author of Hebrews may have just been mistaken in his beliefs. We don't even know for sure if the author was Paul or someone else. It is curious how much weight we put on statements by unknown authors of almost two thousand years ago just because they are part of the Bible. Many if not all of those authors had no idea when they were writing that their letters would be treated as the definitive word of God and included as part of the Bible. Our Life just IS, always has been and always will be. This earth life is just one chapter, and in those terms not the first chapter either. We need to lift our sights beyond the limited context of earth.

There are some horrific accounts of a place called Hell in books and on the internet. Some dying people, a small minority, do seem to see what they think is the Devil and some are convinced they are in Hell, though why they think they deserve it is not clear. One internet site carries the old traditional message that we will go to Hell for eternity if we do not believe in the Lord Jesus Christ. The trouble with that argument is that this automatically includes all the members of other religions as bound for Hell, whether they have done anything to deserve it or not. That amounts to the majority of the human race. The same site confuses the words for the place of death, such as Sheol in the Old Testament, with the later concept of the Lake of Fire. It also says that Jesus went to Hell during his death for us, yet Jesus clearly remarks to his fellow beside him on the cross that he would today be with him in paradise. If we insist on the reality of Hell as a place of torment and retribution we have to be able to say why such a place is necessary. What crime or sin deserves an eternal punishment? Surely such a God who would be that angry would be ignoring the concept of forgiveness. How could a loving God not forgive his own children? Why would a loving God want us to fear him? Fear and Love are opposites. <u>God is Love and is not to be feared</u>. Spiritual progress is not to be had through fear, and those who preach fear are doing much harm to the development of the race.

CHAPTER 15
Hypnotic Regression

Michael Newton, Brian Weiss, Dolores Cannon, and others, from many parts of the world, have conducted and recorded thousands of hypnotic regressions. In these deep hypnotic states people have given accounts not only of their past lives on earth, but their lives between lives in the spirit world. These sessions were being conducted by different hypnotists, unaware of each other, in different parts of the world, and yet the same kind of material emerged in each. As with the other communications there are some variations, and this simply proves that everyone continues as an individual with their own perceptions. Once again the interesting thing is that it doesn't seem to matter what your religion is or whether you have no religion. You enter the Light and are not judged by an all-powerful God. Instead, you judge yourself, reviewing your life vividly in every detail. There are great beings who may be your guides or counsellors who help you to learn the lessons of each life, and to prepare for the next one. Most if not all of these beings appear to have had a cycle of earth lives themselves and are very aware of the difficulties involved. There is no condemnation, yet you do have to face up to yourself and, as we have already seen in my medium sessions, there may be considerable embarrassment or chagrin as you review your actions from such a perspective. Whatever you do here on earth, good and bad, will be reviewed by yourself in the Light. No punishment is meted out, but you will take responsibility for what you have done. When you review your behaviour in that light you actually experience in yourself the effect it had on other people. Punishment is part of our culture on earth, rightly or wrongly, but it is simply not part of that reality beyond. Once again, Hell, as a lake of fire or some other kind of eternal torture, does not exist, according to the stories recounted by thousands of souls. One man who was a hell-fire preacher in one life on earth relives under hypnosis a terrifying trick that his soul group played on him as he returned to the spirit world. They approached him with Devil-like masks on so that he thought he was being ushered into Hell, and he couldn't understand why him after all his preaching. He soon learns that they are teaching him a salutary lesson in a dramatic way. People may put themselves in what can be described as hell while they go through feelings of remorse for violent or criminal behaviour, or even just as a result of intense negative thinking. This hell is psychological in nature, and self-imposed, and the person escapes from it eventually by learning the lesson and forgiving themselves.

The concepts of Heaven and Hell in the Christian religion most likely grew from distorted messages from individuals who communicated their experiences from beyond death. We have to take each communication from beyond as the unique individual experience of each personality. If we were to rely on descriptions of a foreign land on earth to which we have never been, we would find a great variation in opinions. Look at how the witnesses to a road accident can differ in their descriptions of one simple event in time that they all saw happen. Read a selection of opinions from various guests who stayed in a particular hotel, and you might wonder if they were all really in the same establishment. We assume wrongly that when a person passes through physical death they emerge perfect into a perfect world. Why or how would this happen? We are beings who are always evolving and developing in whatever sphere we are in, and we awaken on the other side of death in exactly the same state of mind as when we left earth. Transformation of the soul is by experience; it is not given to us in a magic flash by some other being or God. Consciousness can only develop by coming to know itself. Teachers and guides do help us, but no one can have someone else's experience for them.

In hypnotism it is possible to reach the subconscious mind, and with skill the superconscious mind. The subconscious mind is the part of us that runs our automatic functions and remembers patterns of behaviour that we have laid down as useful. Some of these patterns of course are far from useful, such as smoking, drinking too much alcohol, clinging to phobias, etc. The subconscious mind stores those patterns because it assumes the conscious mind knows what it is doing, and that is why it is hard to break certain habits. The superconscious mind is deeper, and may be described as that part of our consciousness that is aware of our true identity as spirits, the part that looks out at the spirit world. By taking the clients to the superconscious level, accidentally at first, Newton and others found they could describe not only their previous lives, but their previous death experiences, and then their lives between lives in the spirit world. The tunnel experience, described by those who have had near-death-experiences, is also a feature here in these accounts of actual past deaths. Sometimes it is a floating sensation through misty light after being pushed or pulled through the top of the head. The soul travels towards a vast destination with layered levels of light and sound and thought, where it is met by soul mates and guides. Souls are able to recognise each other even without bodily form, but they also have the ability to project whatever form they choose, and can vary this to suit the occasion. Thus a soul who died at an old age could show the form of a twenty-year-old, or a soul who died in childhood and has grown up in the spirit world, could still take the child form to meet a returning parent.

Newton goes on to classify the various learning stages of souls, as beginner, lower intermediate, intermediate, upper intermediate, advanced and highly advanced, and finds a colour range from white through to dark-bluish purple signifying the various levels of advancement. There is too much material to cover here and once again those who are interested should read it for themselves. He himself is wary of being too simplistic in categorising such things, but it raises very interesting possibilities at least. Our soul growth is experiential, and that is why we often experience turmoil and sorrow in our lives. Suffering in itself is not a necessary part of life, and it is not in itself noble to suffer. Yet for many of us it takes a form of suffering to awaken us and to trigger off the process of finding our true origins. This seems to be connected to the great creative experiment on which we as spirits have embarked, namely the creation of the physical human race and its eventual evolution into a new form of spiritual being. Suffering, evil, violence, abuse, psychological problems, are all part of the experience that has accompanied our experiment. Man can only perfect himself by his own struggle, for if he did not, the result would not be genuine. It is a noble struggle. Yet alongside that mighty struggle there is the great power of the Source, the Light, being poured out to help and to guide us. The Bible says it as, "I will pour out my spirit on all flesh" [Joel2:28, and again in Acts2:17]. Many religions including Christianity, have distorted the nature of this mighty struggle and have called it a sinful and self-willed rebellion against God, thus making God angry and disappointed in us. This is the greatest distortion imaginable, and it is really vital that each soul awakens to how wrong that idea is. We are each one of us part of God, or All-That-Is, and we are not in conflict with our Source.

Newton goes on to discover that when we are ready certain guides and teachers help us to prepare for a new life on earth. In an area identified by some as the Ring of Destiny and likened to a movie theatre, the soul can view potential lives and locations. With the help of a guide the soul choses a particular life, as viewed on a kind of living screen or scanner where time can be tracked forwards and backwards or stopped and started. This life is only partly shown, with many scenes or endings withheld, so that there is no sense of the future being completely set in stone. There are many possibilities and probabilities, and this involves the soul continually making choices during the actual future life when it unfolds on earth. This may seem far-fetched at first glance but we need to grasp that time is a tool which is used in different ways and can be manipulated for certain purposes. Remember that souls returning after death to the spirit world tend to see the life just lived on earth as a kind of one-night dream. I myself personally got that confirmed in a medium session. Some of the souls who were present with Rachel described their lives in this way. Time seems to be very elastic. We will see the idea of probabilities and probable selves explained later in the book when we examine the teachings of Seth.

Souls also choose their bodies, according to the descriptions given by those in touch with the superconscious. There is also co-ordination with other souls in our group in setting up the type of relationships they will experience. The choice of body is related to the lessons that the soul is aiming to learn in that life. The body choices made by close soul companions seem to be carefully and skilfully interwoven so that everyone's lessons are set up. Some people who always rub you up the wrong way, for instance, may be there as a deliberate choice, as in a drama, so that lessons are learned or flaws overcome. Once again, comparing the different approach to the same question by Seth, it becomes clearer: Seth says that consciousness creates the body as a manifestation of itself, not just as a container of itself. This seems to me to be a more advanced way of looking at it. People in trance often struggle with how to describe concepts in earth terms. It seems to me that these two approaches coalesce: from a human point of view we seem to choose a body that is offered to us; yet described from the higher dimension of Seth, we are actually forming that body as a manifestation of what we are and what we need to be in that earth life to come. We are always becoming, reaching ever forward to higher levels; having experiences that contribute to the evolution of the soul. Though we reach out towards perfection, in truth we never arrive; perfection would be the end of life and that cannot happen. Creation is endless.

As part of the preparations for an earth life the soul attends another class where certain recognition signals are given. These are embedded and are later triggered on earth when we meet up with significant people who may become spouses or particular friends or colleagues. Most of us would agree that there have been times in our lives when we just "knew" there was something special about someone we may not have met before. I would certainly put my meeting with Rachel in this category, as well as certain other meetings.

We have to think carefully about how much of the information is distorted to some extent by our translating the experience into the physical terms we are familiar with on earth. This does not make the information false or doubtful, but it is good to remember that much of what happens in other dimensions does not necessarily have an exact counterpart in earth terms. Think of it possibly in terms of how a child sees the world as compared to an adult. The child's vision is not faulty, yet it differs from the view of the adult. Readers are urged to explore these sources of evidence for themselves, and many source books are listed in the bibliography at the end of the book. As mentioned before, the biggest lie on earth is that there is no evidence for eternal existence; on the contrary, there is so much evidence available that you couldn't sift it all in one lifetime.

Newton then goes on to explore the idea of our soul groups, to which we return. We each seem to belong to a cluster of souls, maybe around fifteen in number, but again with great variation in this. These close souls tend to have their earth experiences together, and return to further learning in the between-lives state. People describe classrooms, great halls of learning, libraries, and vast buildings. We have to remember that they are translating their experience into earth terms so we might want to be careful about the literal interpretation of it. Yet when somebody describes classical architecture in the spirit world, is it not quite likely that earth architecture is in fact a paler copy of that original? For those who would be put off by the idea of going back to school, it is pointed out that spiritual teachers are wise and benign, and the experience would be much more positive than some of earth school is.

The Council of Elders is another feature that comes up time and again. The elders are apparently the "Old Ones", the "Sacred Masters", the "Venerables", who are not regarded necessarily as the ultimate source of divine authority, but perhaps the highest level for those who are in the reincarnating cycle. Our existence stretches back into unimaginable antiquity; we can only think in terms of time, which we know is not the whole story by any means, but in those terms the great Beings of Light who appear as guides are unbelievably ancient souls. They may well be our "hands-on" creators. They are very compassionate and wise, and they help in reviewing the life just led and in previewing the next life to be embarked on.

The picture is of multiple lives on earth over centuries, interspersed with periods in the spirit realms. Where a hierarchy of souls appears to exist it is based on experience. In the spirit realm you cannot bluff your way as a teacher, for instance. Everything is seen in its true light. Each soul must ultimately learn by its own experiences, but there is always help available, even while on earth. It makes sense; consciousness is experience; no one can give you your own experience, though they may help you through it. We have perhaps entertained the idea of a life of struggle and hardship on this "vale of tears", to be followed by a magical transformation into perfection by an omnipotent God. This does not seem to be the case, and why should it be? If we could be transformed in that way what would be the point in coming to earth in the first place?

Once again, comparing the ideas to the Seth material, what are often termed guides, teachers, coordinators, members of soul groups, or even angels, may from another point of view be the personalities that make up our particular oversoul or entity. The oversoul that sparks us into individual existence is multidimensional. I am not ruling out other guides or helpers by any means, but there may be more to it. A guide that you say has always been with you over many lives may be a closer relative than you think. He or she may be part of your own true inner soul. ✳

CHAPTER 16
Avoiding simplistic theories

There are many who dabble in spiritualism who are content to accept a simple picture of the so-called afterlife. There are regular platform sessions where a medium will get messages for several members of an audience in a spiritualist church or at some other venue. I went to quite a few of such events, though only once did I personally get a message. The message, though vague, seemed genuinely to be from my grandfather, and was very encouraging and I was very pleased. After a few visits, however, I left off. I emphasise that I would not despise these events at all, because to a bereaved person they can and do provide enormous comfort that the loved one is still alive and well. Yet I felt increasingly that I was on a spiritual journey that would go deeper and further than just mere curiosity or comfort. Losing Rachel from the physical plane was such an enormous event in my life that I felt I was meant to make the most of it in terms of spiritual development. Not that my experience of bereavement was any worse than that of all others, but it was my personal experience and therefore it was specifically designed to produce a certain result in me.

Some of the books by well-meaning mediums and would-be mediums seemed to me to be sentimental distortions of a reality that transcends earth existence. There was no standard exactly by which I could judge them, and I may be wrong, but I was learning to trust my instinct. If truth resonates with you, then that is your truth for the moment. There is no lower or higher truth, just a truth that expands as your perception expands. Earth life is just as important as any other phase of eternal existence, but we are mistaken if we assume that other dimensions of existence correspond exactly with this one. Some scientists also often make the amazingly naive assumption that the laws of physics which govern the earth are applicable in the whole cosmos. We know already that there are spectrums of light and sound beyond what we normally experience in everyday life; it is hardly a stretch of imagination to believe that such spectrums are in fact infinite and straddle all realities, perceived in different ways in different worlds. The universe that appears empty to us is in fact teeming with all kinds of life that we cannot perceive. Our own "space" on earth can be occupied by other realities invisible to us.

We project ideas of God according to our earth structures; a powerful male super-figure perhaps, or in a feminist world maybe a powerful superwoman. Other ideas of the nature of a future heaven come from misinterpretations of various sources. For example, Jesus said they do not have marriage in the afterlife: some assume this means no more male or female and no sexual love, yet all he said was that people don't marry. The spirit or soul is both male and female, and in some respects neither, and can take up and lay down whichever form that suits its purpose. Sexual expression is not sinful or base, and the evidence is that it continues in other dimensions after this one, though it is probable that it develops into something much more intense and beautiful.

At times I felt overwhelmed by the search for a clearer version of eternal reality. Rachel's oft-repeated phrase, "You think too much" would echo in my head, but I have never found a way of changing this.I had always wondered even as a child how a loving God could banish his own creatures to everlasting punishment, especially for the so-called crime of not believing in the christian Gospel. Even people who lived good lives would be in Hell because they did not believe. It was absurd. How many parents would banish their wayward children in such a fierce way? Were humans then kinder than their God?

Then there were the constant failures: Adam and Eve in the garden falling from grace through disobedience: mankind then apparently becoming so obnoxious that God wiped most of them out in the flood: Satan as an angel falling from grace and becoming a powerful enemy able to influence man against his God; God sending his only Son to redeem mankind, only to have him crucified and rejected; the Church set up by Christ breaking down soon afterwards. If God indeed was angry with mankind, I reasoned, should he not also take some responsibility for creating faulty workmanship? There had to be a different explanation,--and there is.

So is mankind intrinsically evil? Augustine in the fourth century AD is partly responsible for the idea of Original Sin being accepted as Christian doctrine, although the idea in some form was around long before him. The Apostle Paul in Romans 5 v12, says that sin entered the world through Adam, and death comes to us all because of that. It was the sin of disobedience in Adam's case. But Augustine was by all accounts a sex maniac who was deeply troubled by what he considered as his sinful nature. ["Give me chastity and continence, but not just now", is said to be his prayer when contemplating women.] It seemed to him therefore that everybody is born as the result of sin, the sexual act of intercourse being the expression of sinful lust. Sin entered the world through Adam and we cannot escape it except through God's grace. Our very nature is therefore flawed before we even draw breath.

Our nature is against God who created us. To compound the problem The Devil stirs up our rebellious nature to further influence us to sin and sin again. The relationship between God and Man is one of constant universal conflict. The devil as the powerful enemy of God seeks to score his victory by corrupting man and drawing him into eternal punishment. It doesn't seem to give us much of a fighting chance. Augustine even argued that we should be grateful that God is prepared to save even a minority, so terrible was the sinfulness of mankind as a result of the fall. One of his opposers, Julian of Eclanum, wrote this to Augustine:

"Babies, you say, carry the burden of another's sin, not any of their own... Explain to me then who this person is who sends the innocent to punishment. You answer, God...God, you say, the very one who commends his love to us, who has loved us and not spared his son but handed him over to us, he judges us in this way; he persecutes new born children; he hands over babies to eternal flames because of their bad wills, when he knows that they have not so much formed a will, good or bad...It would show a just and reasonable sense of proprietary to treat you as beneath argument: you have come so far from religious feeling, from civilised standards, so far indeed from common sense, that you think your Lord capable of committing kinds of crime which are hardly found among barbarian tribes."

There are endless arguments about theology, and I had ploughed through many of them when I had earlier struggled to find what I hoped would be the real Church. This is the story of my spiritual journey from fundamentalist Christianity, through confusion and agnosticism, to my own gradual personal enlightenment. It has brought me to a set of spiritual beliefs that my old brethren friends would consider heresy and blasphemy, and it invites the scorn of atheists as well. I often puzzle about why so many atheists get really angry about the idea of eternal life. It is true or it is not true, but why the anger? What is underneath that anger? Why does it bother them? We know that Christians get angry about ideas that don't conform to the traditional heaven and hell and punishment model, but that is sometimes based on concern for the souls who will be "lost" as a result, and also to some extent because the power of clergy and priests is undermined.

This is not a dissection of doctrines, because I soon found that most of the arguments about Christian doctrine were in the end irrelevant to me. I cannot convince the reader of my rightness, or lay out the "Truth". It is simply the account of my own experience and I hope to stir up other individuals to research for themselves, especially for those already disillusioned with both religion and atheism. Many young people especially are put off by the strictures of religion and they fall into the trap of concluding that there is nothing else. I did that for many years, and it blinded me to the fact that life is truly a fabulous, endless adventure, even the "bad" bits. Humans use alcohol and drugs to get away from a perceived reality that we consider boring, pointless, sad, or disappointing. By tuning out in this way we miss the opportunity to rise above ourselves and remember who we truly are.

CHAPTER 17
Darwin

The Darwinian theory of evolution has become an alternative to religious thought and is often seized on by many who have never even read it. When people want to get away from religious dogma it is convenient to find refuge in another theory. Despite being just a theory it has been elevated to definitive truth, and for many it is supposed to rule out God or intelligent design in any form. We are supposed to be beings who developed randomly over millions of years, rising out of some chaotic primeval swamp. Even if this were so it still poses the problem of where the swamp came from. And if we found that out it would still pose another similar question of where that came from. We as earthlings have to have a beginning and an end. Evolution in itself does not rule out the possibility of intelligent design anyway, as it is logical to think that original creations would develop and mature. I had always from childhood found the idea of something without end to be virtually unimaginable. Yet even that was relatively easy somehow when compared to imagining something that has no beginning. What is this thing that has no beginning and end? It is Life, Consciousness, Energy, The Source....call it what you may, you can't deny that it exists. **Yet you cannot find the beginning.** Take a few minutes right now and trace the beginning of all things. No matter how far you go back, you simply can't find it. If there was a big bang, and it looks like there was, **what** was it that went bang? It is unknowable, yet it IS. Pondering on what IS, that has no beginning and no end, is the path to understanding in some way the nature of the Source. You will no longer cling to the simplistic notion that the Big Bang rules out the existence of God.

Darwin was probably more open to new ideas than many of his fanatical modern followers. He was struggling with concepts and evidence that maybe there was no single "God" figure up in heaven who is the hands-on designer of every living thing. To conclude from this that there is no God in any form, or more importantly, beyond our very limited concept of form, is to me a mistake. And then to extend that illogic to state that there is no eternal life is even more of a mistake. Darwin does not supply evidence that would back up those claims. The atheist who looks out at the vast cosmos, even the parts we can see with the naked eye, never mind the infinite realms beyond, and pronounces that there is no intelligent design is surely overreaching himself. Our best instruments have still not detected any boundary to the cosmos, so even if we had sifted all the evidence we can so far detect we still couldn't pronounce on what else might be out there. Imagine a fly on the ceiling of a large house, discussing with other flies whether life exists outside of the room. Some will believe the ceiling is all there is; some will acknowledge the room; some might be daring enough to accept the possible existence of the hallway outside; some will believe the house formed itself at random from a pile of bricks and some conveniently placed cement; the idea of there being a builder is absurd as no one has ever seen him, [it being beyond a fly's ability to see a human being as we see him]; none will realise there is a town or city nearby, never mind that there are acres of land stretching to a sea, which is part of the planet, which is part of the solar system,which is part of a galaxy, of which there are hundreds of billions.... I cannot condemn the atheist, but I personally want to be more open to ideas than that fly. We will come back to Darwinism later in the book, as once again Seth has things to say about him as well.

Science used to be pursued "for the glory of God" and to shed light on the natural order of earthly existence. The Church in medieval times was the supreme power and therefore it largely controlled what scientists were allowed to say. Copernicus in 1543 came up with the idea that the sun is the centre of our solar system, not the earth, and his work was banned by the Church. Giordano Bruno supported him and did his own calculations to show that there were many universes beyond ours, and he was burned to death for heresy. The Church continued to protect its own absolute theories about the universe and inevitably Science gradually grew apart from it. It is a great pity that even today religion and science tend to be enemies, because a coming together would produce much new knowledge. If the church was wrong in its stubborn defence of outdated ideas, so too science took a path of equal arrogance. Descartes in the seventeenth century separated mind and body, and saw the universe and the human body as machines that operated according to mathematical laws. The path that Science took has led us to the amazing technological advances that are still changing our lives, and perhaps it was a necessary evolutionary path for us. The down side of this has been that humanity has lost touch with its spiritual roots to a large degree, with those who cling to an inner knowingness being pilloried as superstitious. The Church in its defensiveness has forbidden the development of free thought, and by thus going into its bunker has left itself looking foolish. At the other extreme most mainstream scientists have assumed the same arrogance as the church, and are denying the spiritual simply because it cannot be calibrated on a measuring device. There are notable exceptions in both camps however, and the purpose of this book is to try and create a bridge so that each individual may escape for themselves off the island of Absolute Truth, over to the mainland of Infinite Possibility.

CHAPTER 18
Ramtha

Ramtha is a being who has been channelled through the woman called J Z Knight since late 1979. He claims to be 35,000 years old, having completed his incarnating cycle on earth, and to be speaking from higher dimensions than even that sphere where most of the recent 'dead' are dwelling. This woman has been tested scientifically to detect fraudulent behaviour. The scientists concluded that although they were unsure of what was actually going on, it was definitely not a trick. I have no proof of who he really is, but most of what he says seems to agree with the other sources of evidence. He teaches that God is everything and in everything. He strongly rejects the idea of an angry and harsh God, saying it is a fiction of man's imagination.

He also claims that it is possible to take the physical body to higher realms, bypassing death, because he himself did that. I still wonder about this statement, though I have learned not to dismiss things just because I don't understand them. In "Conversations with God", by N D Walsch, [page 168], it is said that the death of the physical body was never intended at the outset. In the bible we are told of Enoch, who walked with God and "was not, because God took him." Also Elijah is described going into the heavens on a chariot of fire. In Revelation it speaks of death as the last enemy to be conquered. Ramtha confirms what many energy healers have already discerned, that we have seven bodies in one, each at different vibrational speeds, and relating to various aspects of life. Shedding this visible body we have in everyday life at "death", we then inhabit an astral or mental body in the next phase. The mental body is as solid and knowable in its own sphere as the physical one is here, though lighter and much less limited. It may well be that all this is part of ongoing evolution, and it is not hard to accept that the physical body will eventually not be subject to death either.

To someone like me for whom God had once been an angry taskmaster, this concept of each one of us being Gods, being part of God, and being the creators of our universe, was somewhat alarming. To go from fearing a powerful angry figure in the sky, to thinking there probably is no God, is a major step, but in some ways just a bit of a cop-out. To consider that there is a God after all but it is Myself is quite something else. God is All-That-Is, manifesting in an infinite variety of forms. God manifest in flesh is therefore not just Jesus, but all of us. Jesus did say that we could do what he was doing, and that we would do even greater things. If God is consciousness, consciousness has to express itself, to explore itself, to come to know itself. The myths within most of the religions are saying the same thing. The Adam and Eve story is a parable of man launching out from unknowingness into knowingness. It is not a fall from grace or a fall into sin. Man brought with him the free will to explore all avenues of consciousness, to evolve, to expand in unending creativity. The earth itself in all of its nature is one of the living breathing manifestations of God. Our life did not develop accidentally out of chaos; we are the intelligent creators of our bodies and of everything we see around us.

So who is in charge of my life? I wondered. And the answer came, "I am.". Who do I answer to? Myself. I am God manifest in flesh, yet not confined to flesh or even wholly contained therein. I share this physical existence on earth with all my fellow gods/humans, and we cooperate on deep levels as we evolve the race. Despite some appearances, we are not involved in a struggle against one another. The world holds together because most people cooperate. We are not in a struggle against evil either. There is no force of evil that influences us against God or one another. If I do an evil act it is my own doing; there is no Devil who makes me do it.

My beliefs are not superior or inferior to anyone else's. Beliefs are not static, and in that sense there is no absolute truth. Yet as I open my mind to the god within I find old limiting beliefs fading away. I am not alone, but I am drawing on great gestalts of power and energy from all the dimensions in which I have a part. Individually I know Rachel is alive and still a part of me, while still being her own unique self in full living expression of form in that plane where she currently dwells. She too is multidimensional and exists in many other realities as well as that plane. She has demonstrated that she is still very close to me. I do not own her as a possession of mine, nor did I ever own her, even if I thought I did, but the ties of true love are never ✳ extinguished, and our entanglement will never be unravelled. I do not accept for a second that she has been impersonated by some clever demon who for some reason has nothing better to do. I know what her love feels like and it cannot be faked by some demon. I know that my soul is entwined with her soul, and that we have contributed to each other's development in the life we just had, and probably in other lives as well. That doesn't mean she will spend all of her existence with me, great as that might sound to me at the moment. I would be putting great limitations on her and she on me if we thought that.

CHAPTER 19
The Teachings of Seth

As readers will have gathered, the greatest enlightenment of all eventually came to me through the discovery of the Seth books, partly due to their astonishing detail about all life, and partly because this detail dovetailed so well with all the other sources that I had studied up to now. It confirmed most of Ramtha's material and in many ways went beyond it. It confirmed from a different perspective the descriptions from the mediums, the NDEers, the out-of-body experiencers, and the people under hypnotic regression. If only one avenue of study produced believable results there might be grounds to challenge it, but the fact that all these approaches in their different way point to the very same reality is impossible for me to dismiss. Of course, no amount of evidence will convince a diehard sceptic who is determined not to change. Humans have an enormous capacity to deny reality when they don't wish to accept it. People deny the Nazi holocaust; I knew someone who denied the existence of dinosaurs, despite the literal size of the evidence; some deny the moon landings; it is a world of free will and you are welcome to deny anything you wish. Francis Bacon said, "Man prefers to believe what he prefers to be true." The only proof is personal experience, and nobody has the right to deny another's experience.

Seth is an entity, with many earth lives completed, now evolved beyond the cycle of earth lives, and in a dimension of advanced gestalts of being. He channelled through Jane Roberts from 1963 until 1984. There is an enormous amount of material about God and the universe and all of life set out in impressively precise detail. Seth is a brilliant teacher, yet very strongly opposed to forming any kind of new religion around his teachings. Jane Roberts was most of the time unaware of the material as she spoke in trance, and she would only find out afterwards as she read the notes taken by her husband. Most of what she said was beyond her ordinary knowledge. While she was in trance Seth used her vocal chords, projecting a voice of his own which is quite peculiar to listen to, and nothing like Jane's own voice. Both Jane and her husband were linked to Seth from shared past lives. He often answered questions from witnesses and students. Jane wrote many of her own books as well, detailing her advancing experiences and understandings

THE TEACHINGS OF SETH

of possible and probable realities. The material is so extensive that it requires a lot of study in order to absorb the full meanings of it. It also has a wonderful simplicity to it, however, so it is not difficult in that sense; just that the concepts are so powerful you can go deeper and deeper with each reading.

One theme of Seth's teachings is that we each create our own reality on a daily basis, and the point of power is always in the present. There are many "probable realities" and the life that we know is made up of the ones we choose to experience as we go along. The other probabilities are fulfilled elsewhere in other "probable worlds" by "probable selves". You are a multi-dimensional personality, with a part of your consciousness manifested in flesh and other parts of it alive in other realities. Your physical personality constantly and automatically draws on hidden fields of energy which are infinite. These fields of energy are not impersonal storehouses of knowledge and power, but are gestalts of individualised consciousness. Multiple incarnations in this physical plane which we experience as being one after another in terms of earth years or centuries, are actually in the context of eternity simultaneous. Time is a mere local device for focusing on present experience. Every new personality is a fragment of an oversoul and continues to exist for ever beyond the physical death, taking its own path onwards and joining other great gestalts of consciousness. If "you" were alive in the fourteenth century, for instance, that personality is still alive and contributes to your present self as well as past and future personalities. A 'future' personality may be helping you in your current life from time to time, or even the future part of your present self may communicate with you now. And in a way very difficult for us to grasp, all those personalities from past and present and future <u>are you as a whole</u>. This agrees with the experiences described by the souls meeting up with husbands or wives from various past lives. Seth gives the analogy of the cells of your body: in the same way that all your cells are individually alive in themselves, yet they collectively form your body, so your various incarnations together form the multidimensional you.

In connection with receiving help or information from a future part of me, I remember an incident about a month before Rachel had taken ill. I was not normally demonstrative or gushy, but one day, acting on a sudden powerful impulse, I had pulled Rachel to me as she stood talking to one of the children, and hugged her tightly, telling her how much I loved her. Although no sign of illness had yet occurred, and I simply didn't know why I did this, I later reflected that it was as though my inner soul or a part of my future self had known that I would shortly be parted from her.

Richard Dawkins, in The God Delusion, quotes Julian Baggini's Atheism: A Very Short Introduction:

"What most atheists do believe is that although there is only one kind of

stuff in the universe and it is physical, out of this stuff comes minds, beauty, emotions, moral values--in short the full gamut of phenomena that gives richness to human life."

Although this statement seems logical, it is in fact deeply flawed. He is looking through the wrong end of the telescope. **The mind does not come out of the physical; the physical comes out of the mind.** Consciousness was there first, and it creates the physical. Thought creates reality. Literally. I am frankly astonished at some of the atheistic writers, who try to solve the existence of life from a purely biological viewpoint. They are experts in the science of Biology, but there is far more to life than Biology. For a start, Love is so much greater than mere biology, and the attempt to downgrade it to an irrational urge is amazingly naive to say the least. I shudder to think what that kind of life must be like. Love is the basis for life, Love is Life, Love is God, God is Love. But even if you want to leave out Love, there are the fields of Physics, Chemistry and Psychology, and all of those fields together have a lot to add to Biology. To consider Life from only one point of view is not clever. I was hesitant about commenting on some well known writers because they are reputed to be so clever, but beyond a comprehensive knowledge of Biology I can't see much cleverness in their approach to the origin of life.

Max Planck, one of the most eminent scientists in history, in his Nobel prize speech said:

"All matter originates and exists only by virtue of a force. We must assume behind that force the existence of a conscious and intelligent Mind. This mind is the matrix of all matter."

I don't want to get into the argument about how many scientists were atheists and how many were not, but there were and still are many scientists who are open to the great mysteries of Life.

The entire Cosmos is psychological in essence, even the universe we look out on at night; there is no real division between spirit and material. Material is a manifestation of spirit. A rock is alive in its own consciousness. We already accept that so-called solid objects like tables and chairs are made up of molecules and atoms and electrons spinning in specific vibrations. Consciousness is the source of all "solid" realities. Your body is the materialisation of your spirit into what appears to be solid matter,--it is not just a container of your spirit. The universe that we look out on is not just a collection of pieces of rock and dust, but is the exterior manifestation of Thought in infinite variety, the expression of All-That-Is. God is Thought, All-That-Is, Consciousness, exploding in every direction in order to know itself. Consciousness plays with form, becomes form, yet is not limited to form. The human race is only one of an infinite number of forms and it is still evolving. The notion that there is just man alive on earth and the rest is chaotic emptiness is absurd. As we evolve we struggle with beliefs. That is why we still struggle with what on our level is evil. We are gods developing a new kind of consciousness and we must have free will to experiment. Our gods over the ages have been psychological projections of our nature. Our one omnipotent God has been the projection of our desire to reach a perfect state. The Devil and various demons are creations of our own thoughts arising from fear. Yet although our image of God has been simplistic and possibly distorted, there is undoubtedly a Source of all that we know in existence. **You cannot find the beginning. Yet** the Source of Life IS. This is All-That-Is. The I AM THAT AM that is spoken of in Genesis in the Bible.

Seth teaches that there is one God, but that within that God are many Gods. Similarly, within the one self of the human being there are many selves. We have one body in time, but many other bodies in many other times, as in what we generally call reincarnation. Since time is on one level an illusion, those bodies in other times actually exist simultaneously. We are therefore each one of us multidimensional. Furthermore, even within the one personality we are aware of at any one time, there are many dimensions hidden from the conscious mind. We exist in many dimensions at once. When we sleep we enter a dream world that is just as real as the waking world, and where we work out our path by choosing from a range of probable or possible events. In that sense everything that has happened or will ever happen is already in existence and we simply form our life by choosing from what is out there. There are other probable worlds where the other probabilities are chosen. Every thought and every choice is brought into being somewhere in a probable world by probable selves. This idea in some form has of course been around for a long time.

Seth speaks directly about Darwin and says his theory has no real validity, any more than that of the simple biblical tale in Genesis. He stresses that consciousness is the source of all matter. No matter existed before or without consciousness. No amount of adding to matter or of combining components of matter would ever result in life being evolved. Matter is a dimension of consciousness, and all consciousness is intelligent and creative. Even the ordinary self that we know does not exist entirely within our skin. Energy healers and others have already established this.

Therefore God is within, as Jesus and the other mystics have always said. God is part of the Christian, the Atheist, the Hindu, the Buddhist, the Muslim, and within and part of all things. When you realise that, then you stop looking for an exterior God who tells you what to do, or one who tracks your behaviour. You are responsible for yourself and for what you make of your life. Jesus was challenged about forgiving a man's sins. No one can forgive sins but God alone they murmured against him. Jesus replied, which is easier to say? "Thy sins are forgiven thee", or "Take up thy bed and walk" --six of one and half a dozen of the other. You are not bound by your past, or by a master, you have the power within you to get up and move on. The man was bedridden by his own beliefs, and he had within himself the power to change. Jesus helped him to help himself.

At any stage of our development we should believe what resonates within us. We don't ask children to be adults, and we don't think that children are wrong to believe in certain things that fit their world. Each of us are like children growing up. There is no exterior proof as such, and in order for each soul to develop it has to make its own way. When you are searching for a lost item you have to look in many places where it isn't. It is extremely interesting that some evolutionary atheists have come so close to the reality in some ways, but have managed to miss it by simply getting it all back to front, and by reducing man to a kind of biological machine. Yet this is their current perception, as the children they are, and when they develop they will see beyond their immature ideas. Once you look through the other end of the telescope the view is intelligent and simple. Consciousness, having no beginning and no end, must be the intelligent creator of all exterior form, including what we know as the biological human or animal body. It is, however, not dependent on form for its existence. Thus the human body is consciously laid aside at what we know as death, but the consciousness that was individualised in that body simply moves on to another dimension.

I had at times become very vehemently opposed to my earlier beliefs and even bitter about the EB. It sometimes takes anger to propel you out of something in which you are not being fulfilled. Yet according to Seth and other spiritual teachers, including many of the sources we have discussed here, we see that we actually choose the circumstances of our lives. We choose our parents and our siblings in advance; we choose the country into which we are born; we then choose from a set of possible life paths which will help us to learn and grow. I now accept therefore that I myself chose to be born into that extreme version of Plymouth Brethren, and was aware before I was born that several possibilities were laid out for me to choose from as I grew up. I chose the possibility of that introspective nature, with its drawbacks and its advantages. The path of my life might well have involved me staying with the EB from birth to death. It might have seen me become an atheist. I might have left the EB earlier than I did and missed meeting Rachel. On the other hand we might both have left the EB in our teens and still have met somewhere. Free will exists within a certain prearranged and pre-agreed framework, though this is not the traditional religious idea of Predestination. In that sense, in the greater context, there are no mistakes in life, only experiences as we choose from possibilities. The more enlightened you become, the less dogmatic you are, and you realise that there is so much more still to know; you become compassionate and forgiving; you respect the individual who is different from you. All paths lead to enlightenment eventually.

I am still an unbeliever in Christian terms, but a firm believer in the divine and eternal nature of all life. Christianity is one of the great religions of the world, though quite a recent one, and many people find it meets their needs, and I respect that. It has its own power, but some of it no longer make sense to me. I have seen that life continues in bodily form beyond death, and this seems to me to negate the need for a resurrection of the dead. Why would we resurrect an old worn-out body when we already have a perfectly good one to make the transition at death? Since the old physical bodies have dissolved and returned to the earth anyway, whether by fire or by natural dissolution in the ground or under the sea, the resurrection would have to involve reassembling all the old molecules and atoms of each body from scratch. Whilst that is not impossible by any means, it doesn't seem to have any point to it. Especially in the case of all the sinners apparently destined for Hell!... let's reassemble them and then set them on fire! And surely in the twenty-first century we can let go of that myth as well: a God who would consign his own children to eternal damnation would be by far more monstrous than any of the figures of evil we have conjured up in earth's history, including Stalin and Hitler.

Also, since we are not actually at odds with our creator after all, we don't need to be "saved". This opens up a more beautiful world where we can enjoy being ourselves, each one of us unique and yet closely linked. We all have eternal life as a natural part of who we are; we do not have to earn it or beg for it; we can become aware of our spiritual origins by exploring our inner selves; we love our fellow man; our sense of morality develops through experience rather than through law. It is a pity that many people are put off by the association of spirituality with piety and doomsaying and self-denial. We come to earth and we choose our life in flesh for a purpose, and we are free to enjoy that full experience. Seth is very emphatic that we are not required to deny the flesh. As we take up our freedom we become balanced intellectually, emotionally, and sensually. There is a sense in which you can become lost, by completely forgetting your spiritual origin, being convinced that this life is all there is, and by that means separating yourself from the Source. But you are never lost in the sense of permanent estrangement through "sin", as envisaged by Christian fundamentalists. Jesus spoke of seeking out the lost, and this became distorted to the idea of being eternally lost; yet Jesus was an advanced soul who was here to remind man of his spiritual origins, and to demonstrate that death was not the end but a new beginning.

Religions are often blamed for the violence and wars throughout history, but I think this is facile. Atheistic regimes have been no less cruel in their turn. War is not desirable, but if we consider that individualised consciousness has been and still is evolving over aeons of time, it is not surprising that there will be clashes of free will. War will cease when mankind evolves to a level of understanding which is above Fear. Fear is mankind's biggest enemy. Fear in large part results from man having forgotten his spiritual origins, and therefore to the extent that atheism perpetuates this, it is just as likely to cause more war not less. It may seem that I am condemning atheists more than anyone else; I do respect everyone's right to their beliefs, and atheism is a belief; the most annoying thing about the louder atheists is their smug sense of being smarter than everybody else, when in fact they haven't bothered to look for God outside their own little patch. There is to be no room for mystery and for striving and becoming; everything is cut and dried, labelled and stored away. However, we can't change other people's thinking by just contradicting each other, so all I am urging is for all of us to keep searching with an open mind. The psychological and physical universe is so vast, and the possibilities so countless, that no one can arrive at a definitive answer in one lifetime. Whatever your beliefs are right now, don't close yourself off to new development. Think the unthinkable, and it might not be as unthinkable as you thought.

So what of the EB? In terms of their behaviour in this physical reality, I still think that they are seriously mistaken in their beliefs, and at some level in a future existence they will be embarrassed as they review their lives. Of course, all of us, including myself, will be embarrassed about a lot of things, so they won't be alone in that. They will surely see that separating themselves from the rest of humanity was arrogant. They will surely cringe at the cruelties they inflicted on individuals and families in the name of Truth. I already do; I was an enthusiastic part of the system for some years, and was cruel and unfeeling in many circumstances, sometimes personally, and certainly by group association. Whatever actions any of us are involved in during our lives here, we eventually have to take responsibility for them. Yet the EB members will not be punished. They will in their own way have learned deep lessons from the path they trod, and this will result in an expansion of consciousness, into a deeper capacity for love and compassion. One way to learn intolerance is to suffer it, another way is to inflict it. All those who were born into the EB volunteered for it, as I did, and whether they left it or stayed in it doesn't really matter in the long term. Jesus said in that passage of scripture largely ignored by the EB , "Judge not, that ye be not judged". It was right for me to choose my own path, and to have my own judgment of what I thought was right, but I do not have the right to judge the individual members of the EB for the path they have taken. For a long time I did judge them, but I was wrong to do that. I anticipate that my EB friends and I will have a good laugh about it all when we meet up again and get past the lessons. They of course will be very surprised to see me, as they will expect me to be in Hell, so that might cause some consternation for a while. Hopefully they will not try to withdraw from me again. However, I look forward to seeing my brother and his family again, and to renewing old friendships. If only I could be permitted to kick just some of them in the posterior....but no, better not, and certainly Rachel would probably be appalled at such a thought. Besides, there might be a long queue of people who would have good reason to kick me too, including Rachel herself.

CHAPTER 20
Out of Body Projections

It is impossible to ignore or dismiss the fact that many people have had, and are still having, OBEs, known as out-of-body experiences or astral projections. Some of these are spontaneous and without any apparent trigger. Others have been triggered by trauma or shock. Many others are deliberate excursions by those who have mastered the techniques of consciously travelling out of the physical body. One of the most well known in this category is Robert Monroe, born in Lexington, Kentucky, who learned to manipulate his consciousness in order to go on extensive journeys into the unknown. His first experiences were spontaneous and he spent some time wondering if he had mental problems, but once he got over that he spent the rest of his life exploring the astral realms and established a Mind Research Institute which is still going strong today.

Monroe attempted to map the astral regions based on all his travels. Some believe that he was not actually leaving the physical body behind but was phasing into other realms or dimensions of consciousness. Others believe that we use the etheric body to explore these regions. It is widely accepted that we have seven bodies in one, the physical, the etheric, the mental, the astral or emotional, the Christ Self or Buddhic Body, the Causal or Spiritual body, and the I AM Presence or Monadic body, and each body is related to a specific level of existence. This would agree with the idea of us being multidimensional beings, with a presence in many realities at the same "time". Therefore it hardly matters whether we think of journeys into other dimensions as "travel" in our accepted idea of a journey through space, or whether it is just an expansion of consciousness. Depending on where you are standing it could well be either or both.

These experiences have much in common with near-death-experiences, but often go much further. Those who master the techniques of deliberate projection can go consciously into areas they want to explore, although there are limits. Areas of existence beyond your ability to understand in any way will obviously be blocked to you. It is here that we find confirmation that the cosmos is fundamentally psychological in nature, and that Consciousness, or Thought, does in fact create all realities. Our physical body is designed to function in this specific psychological construct called earth. It is equipped for the purpose; it is in that sense our "spaceship" which houses that part of our consciousness focused on earth. The brain is the transmitter for the mind. Without this body we could not have the full earth experience. Spirits beyond the body, including those who have "died", can visit the physical earth quite freely but cannot enter into it in the full way of those still in physical bodies.

All experience is subjective, and this is a big problem for those who want a definitive picture of the realms beyond our physical existence. There is no fixed objective model for any reality. Every report from the world of spirit all down the ages has been subjective. Ideas that spiritual beings have communicated to earth through the whole history of humanity have all been individualised understandings. In turn, the receivers of those communications have filtered the ideas through their own conscious minds. This accounts for the enormously diverse range of religious and philosophical systems of thought that have grown up through the ages.

Thus you will find astral travellers who describe places that resemble "Hell"; some have found various different "Heavens", including a Christian one. There are many bizarre worlds that have been described. What are we to make of this? I confess that I sometimes become afraid and bewildered by the variety of experiences that people describe. Who is in charge? Is anybody in charge? Suddenly I want to run back to my old certainties where at least I knew what was right and what was wrong. I want somebody to take me by the hand and keep me safe. But I am forgetting that I am part of All-That-Is, that my nature is divine, and that I am consciously connected at many levels with everything that is happening. My physical mind could not cope with the multidimensional complexities of it all. I must trust that my higher self knows what is going on and is able to guide and protect me.

Many of the places described by astral travellers could be probable worlds. According to Seth and others every thought that is generated is fulfilled somewhere, somehow, in some dimension. Monroe described a world where it was full of heaving bodies in endless sexual activities; others have highlighted this to show proof that there is a Hell where sexual sinners are doomed to live out their obsessions for ever. Yet is it not conceivable that there is a psychological or probable world where all sexual fantasies are fulfilled? From what we know about human life it is not hard to imagine that being a very busy world indeed. I only use that as an example. If all thoughts are fulfilled somewhere, then there are worlds where those thoughts become the natives, as it were. Like attracts like and systems are formed. The possibilities are infinite.

I have not so far been able to experience clear conscious journeys into other realities, though I am working on it. We all travel out of body during sleep, but most of what we see or do we cannot remember when we awake. Seth teaches that the world of dreams is just as valid as the waking world we know, and that it doesn't stop when we awake. It is another dimension of our existence. In that sense the dreaming self sees its awake self in the same way as the awake self sees the dreaming self. One feeds into the other. The simplest evidence of this is when you awake with the answer to a problem you couldn't solve the day before. Many inventions are known to have come to scientists in dreams involving astonishing detail.

Whilst a lot of mainstream science rejects all this out of hand, there are many scientists today exploring the possibilities of the various levels of consciousness. All of us can go into the inner stillness of our being and discover for ourselves. A great advance in human consciousness appears to be on the horizon; perhaps a quantum leap in our evolution. People everywhere are becoming more aware, even on everyday levels. Governments are finding it increasingly difficult to hide stuff from us. Communications are getting more and more sophisticated. Science is playing its part, perhaps unwittingly, in opening up new spiritual awareness that will bring true freedom and brotherhood to the world.

CHAPTER 21
The Wings of the Dawn

A nd so I return to one of my favourite Psalms, 139, from which the title
of this book comes. Freed from religion I find the Bible has still a lot of
wisdom and comfort to offer, though I don't regard it as the "Word of God"
in the way I used to. The Bible is a "library" of books, that is what the word
bible means; some of its books contain great wisdom and quite frankly some
don't. It is obvious to us nowadays that stoning people to death for adultery,
for instance, is not a great idea [Deuteronomy 22, v22]. Nor is the instruction
in the previous chapter that involves stoning to death a rebellious son. In
addition, some scriptures have almost certainly been tampered with over
the ages as religious authorities have sought to manipulate the masses. By
quoting this psalm I am not implying it is authoritative wisdom or eternal
truth; it is simply something that still resonates with me as an individual
even after I have gone through the journey of my life to this point. The Bible
may not be the "Word of God", but that is no reason to throw it away in its
entirety.

In my early days as a Christian I found the Psalm moving, yet it was
undoubtedly tinged with my own anxiety and fear of a harsh God. But now
as I read it again I am aware that the God I was looking for was always there
within me, not a harsh taskmaster on high, but a loving and gentle Higher
Self connected to All-That-Is. I do not fear God; I have no reason to fear God.
It is astonishing to think that that last sentence will be regarded as almost
blasphemy by many. But I no longer fear God, and God does not want me to
fear "him". God does not want my worship either. Even as a child I used to
wonder what sort of person would want everybody to chant his praises non-
stop for all eternity. I was afraid to express that such a God must be very vain
and shallow. The God of many of the religions in the world today is paranoid,
very easily offended, burning with anger, and fiercely vindictive. That God
exists only in the imagination of fear-bound men and women. That God is
the creation of man, not the creator of man.

In her excellent book, "God of Jane", Jane Roberts discusses the nature of
God in terms of the Source of All, or All-That-IS, the ultimate source of all
life, and then the idea of a personal and private God that we may turn to for

guidance and help in our lives. She says, on page 65 of this book that I highly recommend:

"This 'God of Jane' idea, or 'God of Jim', or whoever, suits me in many ways. It suggests an intensely personal connection between each individual and the universe, for one thing. For another, it makes important distinctions between the private 'God' and the universal All That Is, while still maintaining the personal involvement. For instance, when I use the phrase "God of Jane", I'm referring to or trying to contact that portion of the universe that is forming me --that is turning some indefinable divinity into this living temporal flesh. I want to avoid all other complications. I'm not trying to contact the God of Abraham, for instance, or the Biblical Christ, or the inexplicable power behind all reality

My intent is more humble than that, more personal, more specific: I want to contact that tiny portion of All That Is that forms my image..."

So, borrowing that concept from Jane, the God of Peter is the part of All That Is which is focused on creating **me.** The greater entity that has sent out a fragment of itself as Peter, is part of All That Is also, but is obviously closer to me in personal terms than the Source of All would be. This entity has sent out its fragment personalities to the physical world, straddling the centuries of earth time, but in another reality operating in the spacious present. In this life I am one manifestation of a multi-dimensional entity, who in turn is part of a greater multidimensional Oversoul. This oversoul is not God in the sense of "God the Source of All", but a gestalt of energy with its own individuality. Yet even when contemplating the Ultimate Source, I do not fear that Source, because it radiates only perfect love.

All of my "past lives" and "future lives" actually happen simultaneously, and each personality is helping the others. I have to let go of my idea of a single-dimensional soul. I am part of an individual Oversoul of immense power. The elders and various teachers and guides that people describe in trance may well be facets of this Oversoul that is individual to each person. It is another view of it, certainly not contradictory, and we must remember to be flexible in how we label things. Some of us alive on earth at this moment may have sprung from the same Oversoul.

So in the Psalm the "Lord" is really your Higher Self, connected to All That Is in ways we probably cannot fully comprehend. It is useful to think of a great Pyramid of power and energy, but a fabulous multi-dimensional pyramid where everything pulses with infinite life, personalised energy cascading down from the Source, and winding through everything in all directions, interweaving in infinite gestalts of being.

This is the Psalm according to the New International translation:

"O Lord you have searched me and you know me.
You know when I sit and when I rise; you perceive my thoughts from afar.
You discern my going out and my lying down; you are familiar with all my ways.
Before a word is on my tongue you know it completely, O Lord.
You hem me in--behind and before; you have laid your hand upon me.
Such knowledge is too wonderful for me, too lofty for me to attain.
Where can I go from your Spirit? Where can I flee from your presence?
If I go up to the heavens you are there; if I make my bed in the depths you are there.
If I rise on the wings of the dawn, if I settle on the far side of the sea,
Even there your hand will guide me, your right hand will hold me fast.
If I say, "Surely the darkness will hide me and the light become night around me",
Even the darkness will not be dark to you; the night will shine like the day,
For darkness is as light to you.
For you created my inmost being; you knit me together in my mother's womb.
I praise you because I am fearfully and wonderfully made; your works are wonderful, I know that full well.
My frame was not hidden from you when I was made in the secret place,
When I was woven together in the depths of the earth,
Your eyes saw my unformed body.
All the days ordained for me were written in your book
Before one of them came to be.
How precious to me are your thoughts, O God,
How vast is the sum of them!
Were I to count them they would outnumber the grains of sand
When I am awake I am still with you...

As my God is my Higher Self, rather than an exterior Lord, it gives the sense of being very close to the immediate source of my being. It recognises that my body is the creation of my Higher Self. And my everyday life, day by day, is created by my Higher Self, filtered through my own conscious mind and beliefs. My God is in the small stuff, the everyday chores, my sitting down and getting up, going to work, mowing the lawn, watching a film, having a shower. All the answers are within. No bible or creed is ever going to give me the answers I need, because I have to find them for myself. No matter what my beliefs are, from fundamentalist Christianity through to atheism, my divine inner self is always with me. I cannot get away from it. I may rise on the wings of the dawn and go as far away as I can, but always my loving higher self is right there with me. It does not follow me--

it is inseparable from me. It created me in the lower parts of the earth; that conscious intelligence formed my body in the womb. Sometimes in my life I have been aware of being "beset behind and before", or hemmed in, and when I stopped kicking against it I found it was my higher self leading me to new and better understandings or new paths. As I look back I can see occasions where the hand of "my God", my own higher intelligence, led me, and times when it held me and saved me from disaster, even when I didn't deserve it. Sometimes I made my bed in the depths, wilfully pursuing my own arrogant path, or choosing to be depressed or bored, and still my higher self remained as my friend and taught me lessons.

Of course, for those who still prefer to visualise an exterior divinity as their guide and source, that is perfectly acceptable as their own personal reality. Names are not important. Divine energy, Divine Thought, is beyond form in its essence, though always delighting in creating and inhabiting the forms it creates. Call the creator by any name you want, you will not be snubbed for using the 'wrong' designation. Our creative source is benign, loving, joyful, and unlimited in potential, and is not to be feared. For Christians, Jesus said, "perfect love casts out fear', and so there is no room for fear in your relations with God. You are loved and cherished and helped in your life even when you may not be aware of it on a conscious level, or even when you might think you don't deserve it.

You can deny your divinity by going as far away as you can from it, and your darkness will still be light; "the night will shine like the day". Yet if you open up your conscious mind to that spiritual stream of energy within, your life will flow more smoothly, and you will never feel like a victim of circumstances. You are the manifestation in flesh of your creator, so there is no conflict; you are both creator and the created in one. You are Spirit dipping into flesh; not falling down into disgrace or sin. You are here for many reasons, one of which is to evolve the human race, and another to evolve your own soul or consciousness. Your flesh is as much part of you as your spirit, and so the flesh is to be enjoyed and cherished, not denied.

By listening to the inner voice, we will find what we know already, and personal life can be enriched beyond either religious or scientific dogma. I have learned during my life to stop listening to experts who have it all figured out. I get frustrated now when I hear the endless arguments about creation versus evolution, as if this has any real meaning or any bearing on whether there is a God. One thing is certain, we will always benefit from opening our minds; there is nothing to fear. The inner self will always protect us. Scientists who advocate banning the creation story, or indeed religious people who try to ban certain activities, do not understand that we come to earth to lose ourselves in the darkness and we become human gods by finding our way out again. If we consider ourselves as victims of circumstances we are missing the point; we choose the circumstances and possibilities in advance

We cannot see the wind, but we see its effects and we know it exists. As Jesus said, it is the same for the Spirit; we cannot see it or measure it with our instruments. We can find it though, if we look inwards. Neither cleric nor scientist can dismiss anyone's unique experience, unless we allow them to do so. Somewhere beyond the intellect in each one of us lies the knowledge of our spiritual origin and home. The intellect of the ego operates at its best when it is in tandem with the inner levels of consciousness. It leads us astray if it focuses only on the factual logic of outward physical manifestations, and when it reduces everything to biology. It is no accident that throughout the ages there have always been sources of inspiration, doors open, windows open, to the world of spirit: visionaries, prophets, mediums, healers, teachers, avatars, hypnotic regression experts, near-death-experiences, out-of-body experiences, and other individual inner knowingness. Of course there have been distortions and misinterpretations along the way, but that does not invalidate the reality of Spirit. There are many enlightened scientists today who are not afraid to look at the startling evidence that upsets past scientific theory. Above all, we are each responsible for our own lives and beliefs, and we should resolve to resist any kind of bullying from those who would limit us.

Time is almost as hard to pin down as life itself. We measure it by the clock and the calendar. Yet even in the simplest terms we all know that "time drags" and "time flies". The effect of time as a substance or force we cannot see is all too obvious on our bodies. A reference in the Bible speaks of a thousand years as one day and a day as a thousand years. Souls in the "afterlife" often speak of their earth life as seeming like a one-night dream. It seems certain that time was created by God or Man as a means of focusing on experience. Consciousness needs to get to know itself, and so we slow everything down so that we can zoom in on specific experiences. A mere flash of eternal consciousness is stretched out into a lifetime of eighty or ninety years. Equally, we can become conscious while dwelling in that lifetime here that we are in that flash of intensity, and that nothing is actually past or gone from us. Consciousness is what we focus on. As we focus our attention in a specific linear fashion events seem to disappear into the past. Yet when we are free of time all those events are perceived as still happening. It is as though we are on earth watching events as on a movie screen. The picture on the screen moves past our point of focus, but it never ceases to be the picture and it doesn't disappear in reality, it just goes temporarily out of sight. Once beyond the physical body we can then see that full movie of our lives in its completeness, including all the good and the bad. As we process the lessons from the mistakes we made we can literally change the screen of events and all guilt is erased.

Seth speaks of "moment-points". It seems to me that moment points are gateways that allow us to enter any possibility or probability in order to explore or experience it. There are infinite numbers of such points, leading out, or perhaps more accurately leading in, in all directions through a psychological universe that includes all form and everything beyond form. My English teacher used to dismiss some of our essays with the quip, "He jumped on his horse and rode off in all directions". I know what he meant; yet now in these terms I do believe we can do just that--ride off in all directions "at once", because we go beyond the world of linear thought and our experience is measured in intensity and in association. In that way billions of souls interweave, swirling through infinite patterns of love and thought, building unimaginably powerful gestalts of being that just fizz with unending creative energy. Each one of us is linked in at many levels with such powerful entities and we can draw on them right now in our earthly life. Perhaps it is all these powerful entities linked together that is the sum total and Synergy of the infinite Power we call God, --and somewhere inside that ineffable Being each one of us can find ourselves.

CHAPTER 22
Does it matter?

Does it matter in practical terms what you believe? Is there any advantage to finding out more about the nature of multidimensional reality? Does life take its own course no matter what you do? There are so many questions.

The answers must be different for every individual. If you feel it doesn't matter at this point in your life, then it doesn't matter. You are correct, though there may come a time when that changes for you. One of those times might be when you experience bereavement. I personally felt so much better when I kicked over my religion and began to live without guilt being foisted on me. The prediction was that I would slide downwards into "sin" and the great horrors of "worldliness". Yet the more relaxed I became about religion the less stress there was internally. The EB would say that I was simply giving in to worldly or sinful instincts, and from their perspective that may have been true. If many things in life are no longer sinful to me then I am not sinning when I do them. Their analysis, however, is based on the old concepts that we are fundamentally sinful and lost from our very birth. I now believe that to be one of the most destructive lies ever perpetrated on mankind. We are in fact completely beautiful beings created out of the very essence of All-That-Is, or of God himself in those simplistic terms that we use.

Even in the context of religious thought, how could it be that an all-powerful loving God would create a perfect world and perfect creatures to inhabit it and then somehow lose control of it? His masterpiece then steadily deteriorates into chaos and failure, and this Omnipotent Creator can do nothing to stop it? Oh yes, well, he can send his only Son to be crucified and take the punishment for all that went wrong... Of course...that makes sense... doesn't it? Inject some Divine Violence into the scene as well, as if there isn't enough. That should help. Unfortunately even that didn't work very well because millions of human beings refused to accept that solution and they are going to have to be burned in eternal hell anyway.

Oh hell, says God, looking around one day, I've really made a mess of this project... and that reminds me...I haven't even created Hell yet, and though I'm tempted at times I never will. And now I'm going to end up with all those Christians who just want to chant my praises endlessly for all eternity. They are lovely people but they aren't much fun at times, always obsessed with their sinful nature. Seems like I offended them by inventing sex and dancing and fun of any kind. I nipped out here to get a break from the praises. And then I turn round and there are the Jews in their own private patch as well. Seems I chose them as my special people at one time. What was I thinking of? I really don't remember saying it at all. Then there are the Muslims, no worse than the rest and I love them all, but quite an angry bunch at times... great. Who are those other crowds?...Hindus...Buddhists....then the ones behind that huge fence?...Exclusive Brethren, who let them in here?! They are Christians apparently but they don't mix with all the others, and they claim to know me personally. Then there's that big cemetery over there...full of atheists who refuse to waken up apparently...they just don't get it at all. And then there's another crowd that hangs around the cemetery gates with their hands in their pockets, agnostics they call themselves, waiting to see what happens. Why do all these religions and non-religions love me and yet hate each other? What part of "Love thy neighbour as Thyself" do they not understand?

Is that the God we want? A god of muddle and mistakes? This version of events is surely an insult to All-That-Is, [or God, Allah, or whatever you want to call him.] God did not create that scenario--we did. What's more, we even created that God. If you sincerely believe in your religion and it fulfils your needs and you are still filled with compassion and love for all humanity, not just your own kind, then by all means stay with it. But if you are left cold by religion and its chaotic creations, and you long for meaning in your life, don't kick out the concept of spirituality as well. That was a mistake which I made, and which many others have also made. As we have discussed earlier, the story of an accidental universe is even dafter than many of the religious ideas, and just as half-baked. It is a scenario once again created by Man, but by the Man who thinks he is separate from All-That-Is; the man who thinks the universe is empty except for him.

There is purpose to earth life. We each have individual purpose, and we are also all part of each other. It is possible and it is intended that we create fulfilling lives, overcoming all the obstacles and challenges that we meet along the way. We are creators and creativity is endless. We collectively created the world as it is now and we do create it anew every day. It would be better if we were moving forward all the time, but sometimes we don't. Seth uses the analogy of a child building with blocks: if the child doesn't like its creation it knocks the blocks aside and builds something new. That is an individual choice. It is not up to me to knock down another's blocks, and in this book I am merely asking for the reader to examine the beliefs he or she holds and to ask why. If your beliefs are not your own, but merely something you accepted from someone else, then they are not serving you in your life.

Your beliefs create your everyday reality. That's why it does matter what you believe. And believing in the fact that life is multidimensional and eternal does provide an important new context for earth life. Earth life is impermanent, temporary, fleeting, but the consciousness that enters into earth life is without beginning and without end. What we do on earth is important, but not that important in the context of the greater universe of which we are part. Material possessions are fine and are to be enjoyed without guilt, but they are temporary props in the drama. The experience of true love is the highest prize. Love expands and deepens. It is the true essence of eternal consciousness. Experiencing true love in many varied situations is what forms the beauty of the soul. The energy that flows from All-That-Is, the Source, is infinite and inexhaustible, and it is Love. The universe is superabundant. Knowing that supplies are inexhaustible would do away with greed and with dishonesty. There is no need to hoard resources when you realise there is more than enough to satisfy every need for every being for all eternity. There is no need to steal from others when there is enough for everybody.

Forgiveness and compassion are essential components of love, so there is no need to focus so intensely on blame and guilt and punishment. We would find new and better ways to deal with those who transgress the rules of society. Compensation lawyers would go out of business, poor souls, but we could set up a fund for them. In the context of which we speak there are no victims. Each of us draws the experience we need to us. We are responsible for ourselves.

Personally therefore I think it is worth knowing that life is eternal and that there is no rift between man and "God". As unique individuals we are creators of new life. We do not need to worship or revere gurus and teachers and priests, nor even the Source itself, or form new religions in place of old ones. Once we have opened our minds to the wider realities we are free to create and enjoy earth life to the full, because that is the very reason we came here. In times of testing and grief we can gain some comfort in knowing that there is much more to our existence than the narrow focus of this one earth life.

I can only speculate about the reasons for grief and sadness being part of our earth existence. It has been said that without the darker moments we would not be able to fully treasure the lighter moments. We need the contrast in order to really know the experience. This is one reason. Robert Monroe had a theory that the quality of emotion that is generated by earth experience is unique in the universe, and he wondered, perhaps tongue in cheek, whether we are being milked like cows for that priceless substance.

I personally think there is a grain of truth in that, though we are not animals in a cosmic farm. In the Seth books we come across a being that was labelled Seth Two, who appears as a powerful entity far removed from our understanding, and beyond the level of Seth One. Yet he also admits he does not really understand earth life in spite of the fact that he was among those who seeded earth in antiquity. He appears cold and emotionless in our terms, though he does express some loving sentiments in words towards us. I find it credible that Consciousness, having exploded in all directions, has taken so many different paths of development that in its outer reaches its parts appear quite alien to each other. Many of these "aliens" [to us] may be more advanced in many ways than we are, but in the matter of emotion they may be less developed. Both the Seths say that no level of consciousness is superior to another, just different. Perhaps the greatest development of the human being is emotional consciousness of a quality just not seen elsewhere in the cosmos. The depths of agonising experiences we go through on the one hand, from the result of war, crime, abuse, tyranny, famine, and all kinds of what we call "evil", plus bereavement, coupled with the high levels of joy and fulfilment on the other hand that we experience in relationships and creativity and fun, all lead to the formation of a unique and beautiful kind of "being". As mankind evolves through the stages of his being he becomes a truly incredible loving species that is rightly admired by all the rest of the cosmos. When I say "he" I gladly include "she", male and female being equal in every way yet both contributing something unique and special. Since time as we know it is an illusion this is already a fact. We are simply in the process of growing into our "future", which, paradoxically, we are also creating as we go along.

THE END

*You are welcome to contact the author by emailing: pjmccormack20@hotmail.com

BIBLIOGRAPHY

Seth Books, by Jane Roberts:
The Seth Material
Seth Speaks: The Eternal Validity of
the Soul
The Nature of Personal Reality
The Individual and the Nature of
Mass Events
The Magical Approach
The Nature of the Psyche
The Unknown Reality
Dreams, Evolution and Value
Fulfilment
The Way Towards Health

Jane Roberts
God of Jane

Ramtha
The White Book

**On Hypnotic Regression to past
lives and beyond:**
Michael Newton:
Journey of Souls
Destiny of Souls

Brian Weiss
Many Lives, Many Masters
Same Soul, Many Bodies

Dolores Cannon
Between Death and Life

 For Near-Death experiences:

Raymond Moody:
Life after Life

The Light Beyond

Kenneth Ring
The Omega Project
Mindsight
Heading Towards Omega

For scientific connections:

What The Bleep Do We Know?,
[both book and DVD]